THE LION'S
PRIDE

THE LION'S PRIDE

AMERICA AND THE
PEACEABLE COMMUNITY

Leonard I. Sweet

Abingdon Press

Nashville

The Lion's Pride: America and the Peaceable Community

Copyright © 1987 by Abingdon Press

This book is printed on acid-free paper.

Library of Congress Cataloging-in-Publication Data

Sweet, Leonard I.
  The lion's pride.

  1. Peace—Religious aspects—Christianity. 2. War—Religious aspects—Christianity. I. Title.
          BT736.4.S94   1987   261.8'73   87-12560
          ISBN 0-687-21857-8 (alk. paper)

"Ultima Ratio Regum" reprinted from *Collected Poems 1928–1985* by Stephen Spender. Copyright © 1986 by Random House.

"What Will You Do, God, When I Die?" by Ranier Maria Rilke reprinted from *Poems from the Book of Hours.* Copyright 1941 by New Directions Publishing Corporation.

Scripture quotations unless otherwise marked are from *The New English Bible.* Copyright © the Delegates of the Oxford University Press and the Syndics of the Cambridge University Press, 1970. Reprinted by permission.

Scripture quotations marked NIV are from the *Holy Bible, New International Version.* Copyright © 1973, 1978, International Bible Society. Used by permission of Zondervan Bible Publishers.

Scripture quotations marked NKJV are from The New King James Version. Copyright © 1979, 1980, 1982, Thomas Nelson, Inc., Publishers. Used by permission.

Scripture quotations marked RSV are from the Revised Standard Version of the Bible, copyrighted © 1946, 1952, © 1971, 1973 by the Division of Christian Education of the National Council of the Churches of Christ in the U.S.A., and are used by permission.

Scripture quotations marked NJB are from *The New Jerusalem Bible,* copyright © 1985 by Darton, Longman & Todd, Ltd. and Doubleday & Company, Inc. Reprinted by permission of the publisher.

Manufactured by the Parthenon Press at
Nashville, Tennessee, United States of America

Contents

To Leonard I. Sweet, Jr.
. . . and let it begin with me . . .

Acknowledgments

Acknowledgments are a time when you introduce the people who came here with you—people who risk their reputation by sitting next to you, being seen with you, and staying with you when everyone else walks out. At greatest risk is Professor Marion T. Soards, associate professor of New Testament at United Theological Seminary. Marty read and critiqued this book while keeping his keen, trained eye out for fuzzy, untrained interpretations of biblical passages. He has used every technique in the book—harassment, intimidation, humiliation, and threat—to tighten the harness while I rollicked on a loose rein through the Scriptures. Some of the time his restraints were successful, and even when I did not obey, I tried to observe. He will be glad to see that I have relinquished hold of one interpretation of a Pauline text. Actually, I had little choice, since he threatened to denounce me publicly if I kept it in (I still think I am right). But whatever this book's value, it would have been a much less useful and sound one without his good-hearted gibing, jabbing, and severe scrutiny of my biblical exegesis.

This book is a left-handed piece of work, written in response to invitations to address the theme of peace. I could not have accepted nearly as many of these invitations without the presence in my life of Betty O'Brien, my right arm and left brain. Betty knows what is in this book better than I do. If ever there were the scholar's dream of an ideal research assistant, Betty is that one. I believe God sent her to me, and even though she seldom has a nice thing to say about anything I write, my life would be seriously handicapped without her.

The third of four persons to have read this little book in its entirety is Karen Elizabeth Rennie, Ph.D. candidate in history at the University of Rochester. Elizabeth has proved many times the truth of Schleiermacher's paradox: A text is more deeply understood by its reader than by its author. Elizabeth encouraged me to take intellectual and spiritual possession of many of my musings, while her doubts helped to keep my faith from getting red. If any reader wishes I were less meager with metaphors, you can blame Elizabeth. She put my prose on a restricted diet, thus limiting the amount of images taken into the text.

Finally, my secretary, Ruth Wert, typed drafts of this thing more times than she wishes to be reminded. In working for me these past couple of years I don't think she has ever been certain whether she is foolish, fooled, or fooling with a fool. I'm not about to tell her now. Ruth has cyclopean sense of what is needed in the struggle between the mind and manuscript paper. Most of all, Ruth's faith has what Marianne Moore once called fiber: It is strong and flexible. Her fibrous piety shored up my weaker strands many a time.

This book would have assumed a very different form without conversations with friends and editors. Marie Aull is the closest thing I have to a guru. In turning me from my own creative obsessions to God's, she has tutored me in the art of identifying the tracks of God, from sky to sod. She has also taught me that writers stand in need of more forgiveness than others, for the birth of a book requires the death of a tree. Whether this book is worth the trees it killed is problematic. Stan Brown portrayed, in one of his masterful sermons, the relevance of the Garden of Gethsemane for a shalom community. Sue Schantz's three-page, single-spaced critical reflections on two lectures delivered at METHESCO put a tail on my kite just when it started to soar out of sight. The editorial interventions of Michael Lawrence and Rebecca Marnhout have kept many blemishes from becoming disfigurements.

My eight-year-old son Justin did not read one word of this book, but he helped write it, both literally and figuratively. He jotted down for me some things he knew about children's culture and his feelings about the bomb, that found their way into the text. And he taught me that nothing is theologically weightless—one can make theology out of a "Garbage Pail Kid" (as Justin would express it) or a glass of beer (as Martin Luther would have put it).

It is because of this lesson learned at the feet of a child that I have been able to think through this topic of war and violence without ending on the familiar note of gloom or getting to the place where humanity's only hope seems to be in pressing every button we've got, in hopes that one of them will produce the desired effect. But ultimately it is only two pieces of wood that prevent me from thinking, saying, and doing just that.

Introduction

We are the generation that stands between the fires. Behind us
is the flame and smoke that rose from Auschwitz and from
Hiroshima. Before us is the vision of a Flood of Fire: a
thermonuclear holocaust that could make every human city a
crematorium without a chimney. It is our task to make from
fire not an all-consuming blaze but the light in which we see
each other; all of us different, all of us made in the image of
God. We light this fire, to see more clearly that the earth, the
human race, is not for burning. We light this fire to see more
clearly the rainbow in our many-colored faces.
—from "Rainbow Liturgy for Seder," Shalom Peace Center

Samuil Marshak, the Soviet writer of children's books, was
child-sitting six- and seven-year-olds one day. "What are you
playing?" he asked them. The children replied, "We are
playing at war." "How could you possibly play at war?" said
Marshak. "You know war is bad. You should play at peace."
"That's a good idea," said the children. Then there was a
silence, whispering, and again silence. At last one child spoke
up: "Granddad, how do you play at peace?"

The transformation of killing fields into playing fields
stands as the ultimate dilemma for these twilight years of the
twentieth century. How do you play at peace? We've entered
another season of what poet Robert Lowell once called
somewhere "the reign of piety and iron." "The only thing
keeping America alive today," one of America's most

important military leaders told me, "is God and military power." *The Lion's Pride* explores the dynamics of piety and iron, the relationships between the two major issues facing this bloody, battered, broken-down century as it draws to a close—religion and war. My role in this book is much like Fay Weldon's image of the writer in *Rebecca West* (1985), poking his or her head "out of the trench of anonymity, to look around at the war zone which is the world," then reporting back with "excited incredulity," drawing sniper fire in the process. For example, I feel such things as President Reagan's famous 1984 faux pas, spoken into a live microphone ("My fellow Americans, I am pleased to tell you that I have signed legislation to outlaw Russia forever. We begin bombing in five minutes.") must be reported and examined. *Not* coincidentally, this announcement occurred while the president was conducting a voice test for another announcement: "I am pleased to tell you that today I signed legislation that will allow student religious groups to begin enjoying a right they have long been denied—the freedom to meet in public high schools during nonschool hours." The need to decode the connections between piety and war is, if possible, greater now than it has ever been.

This book began life as a series of four lectures delivered at the 1986 Ministers' Week conference at Lake Junaluska, North Carolina, which had as its theme "The Bible and Peacemaking." The series could also have been called "Into the Word and into the World." The organizers of the conference believed that the church's thinking on war and peace needed some transfusions from the Bible. Upon their invitation I agreed to reread the Bible, to the end of developing biblical perspectives on war and peace. My method of biblical interpretation was stolen from George Herbert, who in the words of his biographer brought "to his study of the text that minute absorption with which we examine ourselves in the mirror, that attention with which we read whatever is written about us: it is his mirror, his story."[1] During Ministers' Week, I discovered that what had become, in the course of my research, my mirror and my story, would not be fully complete until it became our mirror and our story.

I left Lake Junaluska convinced of the importance of experiences like that of the young Francis of Assisi, when he fled to a cave after his failed and humiliating military campaign had sunk him into a deep depression. G. K. Chesterton, whose little biography of Francis describes this incident, says that during this cave experience something special happened, and that Francis became such a new being that he exited the cave as if he were "walking on his hands."[2] His world had been turned upside down; he had rethought old patterns until life was seen from a totally new perspective. He had broken the war habit. He began to think what Jeremiah called "thoughts of peace" rather than "thoughts of war." That is my hope and prayer for you, as for me, in the course of this book.

Peace thoughts require that peace research be conducted with what Jesuit theologian Richard T. McSorley calls "peace eyes."[3] *The Lion's Pride* aims at developing the ability to read the Bible with "peace eyes," or as Saint John of the Cross called it, "seeing with the eyes of a dove." The subject of this book can hardly be described, in the words of a college student's essay, as a "virgin field, pregnant with opportunity." The stockpiling of books on peace, like the production of nuclear weapons, keeps getting bigger. In the 1980s especially, a wide assortment of authors have found in peace, war, the arms race, and the church and the bomb, something to get heated about. Truly, every one of these issues is a passionate matter. Each will bring in letters to the editor faster than one can print in a newspaper the words "dog control."

My purpose is not to bring to the discussion a dash of cold water. Just the opposite. In a society with a mayonnaise-jar mentality ("keep cool, but do not freeze"), somebody needs to keep the pot on boil. We continue to display the unique capacity of talking a lot about peace while at the same time taking big steps toward war. This makes the need for someone to tend the stove all the more pressing, especially when the prevailing menus for peace call for SALT-less recipes. Where our arguments have not been brought to a simmer, much less a boil, my hope is to provide more heat. Cold water is sprinkled liberally on issues only to keep the discussion from boiling over.

Peace is seen in this book from planes placed beyond the conventional, jargon-filled categories, the foreground tilting forward to reveal complex historical realities usually crammed into background schemas, and the angle of perspective changing as the discussion moves on and through the subject. But the drama of piety and iron and its vast range of characters are always placed squarely within the world in which American values and traditions operate. I have done this for three reasons. First, the distinctively American context, which brings together religion and war, has not been adequately acknowledged or explored by either secular polemologists (professionals who study war and peace) or religious prophets (peace activists, theologians, rabbis, and pastors). Second, the biblical message of peace possesses amazing ventriloquism talents. Until peace is allowed to speak out of the mouth of the American character, it will not penetrate hearts armored against all sentiments which disdain or disregard patriotic feeling. Finally, America has been called to a special peace mission. Because of "the baptism of the atomic bomb," Japanese scholar Yasuo C. Furuya writes, American and Japanese Christians have a common mission. Indeed, "it is not an exaggeration to say that world peace and the survival of humankind depend on American Christians."[4]

Will they ever lie down together: the lion and the lamb, the sheep and the wolf, the tiger and the turkey, the hawk and the dove, the eagle and the bear? The Lion of Judah is calling American Christians and Jews to build a peaceable community. To a far greater degree than we want, or is safe, the Lion's pride depends on us.

CHAPTER 1

Not All Geese
Are Swans

When nothing else turns up, clubs are trumps.
—Thomas Hobbes

The first promise of the atomic age is that it can make some nightmares come true. The capacity so painfully acquired by normal men to distinguish between sleep, delusion, hallucination and the objective reality of waking life has for the first time in human history been seriously weakened.
—Edward Glover, *War, Sadism & Pacifism*

American religion's "new awakening" to the peace agenda is one of the most salient features of contemporary church history. During the 1980s—a period of history dominated by a mentality of "exterminism" (historian E. P. Thompson[1]), the ordained, adored virtues of a military society came back into vogue—indomitability, prowess, stoicism, macho power. Yet during this period America's oldline (i.e., mainline) churches, Roman Catholics, and even some parts of the new evangelical establishment have labored hard to get the church back under the peace flag. Even more important, statements on peace like *In Defense of Creation* (1986, United Methodist), *Seeking God's Peace in a Nuclear Age* (1985, Christian Church [Disciples of Christ]), *Peace and Politics* (1984, Lutheran Church in America), *The Challenge of Peace* (1983, Roman Catholic), *Mandate for Peacemaking* (1982, American Lutheran Church), *To Make Peace* (1982, Episcopal Church), *Before It's Too Late* (1981, World Council of

Churches), "Christian Imperatives for Peacemaking" (1981, Reformed Church in America), *Peacemaking: The Believer's Calling* (1980, United Presbyterian Church in the U.S.A.), and *New Call to Peacemaking* (1976, Quakers, Mennonites, Brethren) represent denominational and ecumenical circles exerting moral authority in the cause of peace by advancing and clarifying our thinking about war.[2] The pastoral letter and foundation document of the United Methodist Council of Bishops, *In Defense of Creation,* for example, is not just a landmark ecclesiastical document. It is also a landmark action-study guide written by those whom H. G. Wells accused of being "always socially in evidence, and intellectually in hiding," which shoves forward public discourse about peacemaking and removes much that is unclear from what is nuclear. Since the early 1980s, the freshest and most significant theological reflection on war and peace have come not from academic theologians but from bishops and ecclesiastical task forces.

All has not been said and done, however. First of all, the major faiths should now get together and draft something as comprehensive and forward-looking as the Brandt Commission Report (*North-South: A Programme for Survival,* 1980) to confront the divisions that separate them and to combine their resistance to the principalities and powers that threaten the earth. Second, there needs to be an exploration of war and peace within the horizon in which our cultural values operate. None of the official statements on peace by councils of bishops or denominational or ecumenical assemblies addresses the distinctive voice of America through its civil religion and civil eschatology. It is not enough just to read the Bible of our faith religion with "peace eyes." We must also learn to read the Bible of our civil religion with "peace eyes." I begin this study by turning my own "peace eyes"—and I confess that I am still an infant at the vocation of seeing with them—on a portion of the scriptures of American civil religion. I begin very personally by relating a dream I had a few years ago, a dream which made me "walk on my hands."

Safely burrowed away for a month at a friend's home in Toronto, I paused one afternoon to paw through a pile of periodicals I had carted with me. After a couple of hours I began fighting sleep, and just before I succumbed I picked up an old article in *Commonweal* by Harvard's David Riesman, entitled "The Overriding Issue."[3] Riesman's thesis was straightforward: The paramount task for the rest of this century is the avoidance of a nuclear holocaust. Could it be, I mused drowsily, that the amassing of nuclear armaments stands as the greatest moral issue of our time, and indeed the most dangerous one, as we approach the twenty-first century?

The next thing I remember, I was standing in the Japanese garden of an ultramodern home, pruning a bonsai tree. My young son, Justin, was playing by himself on a red brick patio with his toy tractor, and I heard in the background voices from the house. I continued pruning but muttered to myself about how people can be full of surprises. The last I knew of myself, and where I lived, I had made my peace with weeds, was not enamored of Japanese art, owned a home built in 1840, and collected antiques.

Suddenly the sky lit up with a pinkish light, followed by the most dazzling display of fireworks I had ever seen. I knew immediately that these were the fireworks of the Apocalypse, but my first thought was as unreal as the sight I was witnessing. My dispensationalist friends had turned out to be half-right, I mused: Those who were alive and remained were going up in a cloud as they had predicted, but it was a mushroom cloud.

I could not take my eyes off the heavens. I stood hypnotized by the sight of colors in battle, with sky blue being easily beaten back by the underworld forces of red-orange-yellow. When the last vestige of blue had been driven from the heavens, my eyes dropped to the horizon, where I first saw the atomic volcano erupting and the tidal wave of lava, the molten remains of a planet's life, rolling down our street. My first instinct was to run into the house and warn everyone. But before my feet could respond to my brain's impulses, I watched helplessly in horror as my home and everything in it was petrified, like the city of Pompeii, by the literal cinders of civilization.

The happy sound of "vrrumm-vrrumm" startled me. I looked around at its source and saw my young son still playing contentedly, blissfully unaware that at that instant a lava wave had cupped over him. The hatred for all government that surged through me at that moment, and the kinship I felt with every Russian family, are indescribable and unperishable. As my mind crumbled into insanity, I became a total blank except for these words: "Give me liberty or give me death." Before the lava crashed upon me, I screamed with an unsurpassed hatred, "Who gave you the right? Is anything worth this price?"

I awoke, instantly aware that I had just been exposed to (and you have just read) pornography—for to describe nuclear destruction is to commit an obscenity: to display what should never see the light of day, to make a show of what should never be shown, to represent and thereby recognize a world that is beyond representation and recognition. Because of that pornographic nuclear nightmare, my nights and days have never been the same. All dreaming now requires exceptional courage and determination. For dreaming, like the questions and jokes of children, has lost its innocence. A comic strip by Lynn Johnston found in *Peace Notes* conveys this lost innocence with convincing simplicity. In the first box, a child sitting on the lap of his father says: "If there was a bomb dropped on us, Daddy . . . would we go to heaven?" The child continues in the second box: "Would heaven get filled up? Would everyone turn into angels?" In the third box the child, still speaking, adds: "And what about the people who dropped the bomb? Would they be alone on the whole earth?" The fourth box has the dad hugging the child and saying: "Mike, can we go back to 'Why is the sky blue?' "[4]

Even children's knock-knock jokes have entered the no-laughing-matter nuclear age: "Knock, knock." "Who's there?" No answer.

History students have the easiest time identifying these three speeches in American history: Martin Luther King, Jr.'s, "I Have a Dream" Washington Address, Abraham Lincoln's "Four-score and Seven" Gettysburg Address, and Patrick Henry's "Give Me Liberty or Give Me Death" speech. But of the three, Henry's March 23, 1775, speech before the Second Virginia Convention, summoning Virginia to declare a state of defense and to arm for an "inevitable" war that "we must fight!" is the most recognizable. This oratorical classic has as honored a place in the bible of our civil religion as John 3:16 has in the Bible of our faith religion. It is part of our common identity and heritage. The sentiments it expresses rush through the veins of every red-blooded American boy and girl. "Give me liberty or give me death!" is sculpted into the soul of America.

It is becoming more and more apparent that the "give me liberty or give me death" ideology is dangerously inappropriate to a world possessing nuclear technology. Indeed, the nuclear age is without a usable past for dealing with war and peace. In Albert Einstein's not-too-often quoted words, after the birth of nuclear power everything changed except the way we think.[5] We need not stop thinking "live free or die." But red-and-white-and-blue eloquence and dragonfly thinking—gleaming, metallic, darting, and fragile—are false foundations on which to build either a defense or a deterrence policy based on nuclear weapons. If it is true, as J. G. Fichte argued in the eighteenth century, that what we choose to believe determines what we will be, then we had better be careful about our philosophical assumptions and arguments.

Most of our arguments for the arms race forget that not all geese are swans. Our arguments pitting America against Russia sound intelligent and look impressive. But they are based on dodgy logic, counterfeit issues, and frequently squeeze out the last drop of meaning from dying clichés.[6] They are like the intelligently stupid logic of the person who reasoned: "When we were married, my spouse was thirty and I was eighteen. My spouse is now sixty years of age or twice as old now as then. So I must be thirty-six." In moral terms, they are often the equivalent of a geographer saying that Denver is to the left of Chicago.

One of the most important but least studied aspects of history is the proneness of people in every era to tell little lies when they ought to be telling big truths. In fact, one day I hope to do a book with the title *The History of Lies*. It will take a look at such things as Freud's observation that during war home populations become massively depressed, a fact he attributed in part to the sudden social sanctioning of lies. It will explore the connections between depression as our current "common cold of mental illness" and a society saturated in media "hyperism" and hucksterism. It will seek to understand the "heavenly deceit" phenomenon, whereby "any lie will do in the service of truth." The longest chapter, however, will be devoted to the ideology of nuclearism, one of the most dangerous conceptual deceptions ever played on society and the church. For in the nuclear arms race, we are financing some of the biggest fantasies and horror stories this world has ever seen.

The trajectory of thought traces the history of the heart. Or as Karl Barth used to say, "The crooked man thinks crookedly." We are so crooked in our thinking about peace that if we swallowed a nail we would pass a corkscrew. Nine out of ten Americans believe a nuclear war is unwinnable, yet the majority of Americans support "new and better nuclear weapons." Eight out of ten Americans believe that "there is nothing on earth that could justify the all-out use of nuclear weapons." Yet the majority of Americans would be "willing to risk the destruction of the United States rather than be dominated by Russia," and over two-thirds oppose a U.S. policy of never using nuclear weapons.[7] Given this dizzying disarray of thought, one can understand how some have concluded that nuclear armaments have become for nations what alcohol is to the alcoholic.[8]

A couple of examples from the no-war movement and from the just-war movement reveal how the rigging of even our best reasoning on war and peace can be flawed and dangerous. The no-war movement is preoccupied with the evils of the nuclear bomb. But in the not-so-distant future the bomb will be an anachronism, trashed by technological forces moving so fast that it has become an axiom of the military R & D establishment that "if it works, it's obsolete." Further, as *Dr. Strangelove* (1963) has reminded us for the past two decades, the real doomsday machine is not the bomb but human beings themselves. "What causes wars, and what causes fightings among you?" asks the apostle James. He replies: "Is it not your passions that are at war in your members? You desire and do not have; so you kill. And you covet and cannot obtain; so you fight and wage war" (James 4:1-2 RSV). The UNESCO charter states flatly, "Wars begin in the minds of men." The bomb is a product of selfishness and sin. War is a consequence (although not an inevitable one) of human sinfulness.

Finally, the bomb is not inherently evil. Matter is not evil, not even the nuclear bomb. In fact, our knowledge of how to create the bomb is good. Aquinas taught us clearly and convincingly that the knowledge of anything evil is *itself* good. American technology is not in and of itself evil. Evil comes from what one does with American technology, from whether one decides to make a world-ending weapon or a space station. The issue is not the abundance of our ABC weaponry (atomic, biological, chemical), but the dearth of ABC theology (anointed, biblical, Christocentric) and in our lack of a spirituality of technology. James Turner Johnson's *Can Modern War Be Just?* contends: "It is not the weapons of war in our time but the assumptions about war that are morally questionable. Weapons are but tools of human intentions, and the reason we now live in a world where entire populations are threatened by nuclear missiles is that we have come to regard such thinking as appropriate."[9] The fundamental problem is not weaponry, but arguments, ideas, thinking, and theology. Mortal problems must have moral answers; theological dilemmas require theological solutions.

Now some examples of thought from the just-war movement. Most people who are not NUTS (nuclear-use theorists) or MAD (mutually assured destructionists) or INSANE (instant-strike-anticipating-nuclear-exchange) will concede to war on the grounds of just-war theory. In spite of the terrible lessons of World War I, World War II, Korea, and Vietnam, we have plainly learned nothing. Once again, this nation that does not look back, and looks ahead only two feet, has not profited from its past. One almost concludes that the dead have, in Abraham Lincoln's words at Gettysburg, "died in vain." What have all the wars of the twentieth century taught us? Certainly not the meaning of peace. Actually, this should not surprise us as much as it does, for the idea that experience is a good teacher is one of the silliest obsessions in human history. If it were true, perfection would have been ours long ago. "Learning teacheth more in one year than experience in twenty; and learning teacheth safely, when experience maketh more miserable, than wise," wrote Roger Ascham in *The Schoolmaster* (1570). We still repeat all the meaningless phrases about national security, and have even developed a secular theology of security with a defense dogmatics at its heart, called nuclear deterrence.

The whole philosophical foundation of deterrence is based on the premise that the human race is to be preserved from annihilation by threatening to annihilate the human race. Men and women of faith have mindlessly bought into a system in which it is morally right to threaten to do something immoral. It seems that the Pentagon has become the most religious place in America, for it is the place where we all leave our religion. Strangers to the ways of God have held our brains in their hands too long. It is time we took them back and joined with seventeenth-century theologian Jeremy Taylor in saying about the notion that the end justifies the means:

> But when a man does evil that good may come of it, or good to an evil purpose, that man does like him that rolls himelf in thorns that he may sleep easily; he roasts himself in the fire, that he may quench his thirst with his own sweat; he turns his face to the east, that he may go to bed with the sun.[10]

To brake the logic that pushes the arms race forward will take a whole new logic, a whole new way of thinking. It will take theological statecraft and a biblical approach to the world.

Genesis was right. War is a theological problem. It is not a political, or economic, or sociological problem. The four basic problems of human existence that beset Adam and Eve—sex, greed, pride, and violence—are all profoundly spiritual issues. The story is told that during the Middle Ages two warriors wearing full armor were riding through the countryside on horseback, each thinking that there was no one else for miles around. They came upon each other in a particularly dark spot. Both were startled and each mis-judged the movements of the other as signs of hostility, so they began to fight, each believing that he was under attack and that he had to defend himself. As the conflict grew in intensity, one of the warriors managed to knock the other from his horse, whereupon he drove his lance through his opponent's heart. The victor dismounted and bent over the man he had killed. He pulled back the dead man's facemask, and to his horror, he recognized his own brother. We are all children of Cain, for Abel left no descendants.

As King David discovered to his horror (II Samuel 11:24–19:4), the battle can be won, the enemy vanquished, but the victory tastes like ashes and joy turns to mourning when a beloved son is dead. Every war pits brother against sister, sister against brother. Pablo Picasso's *Guernica,* Ernst Barlach's *Magdeburg Memorial* sculpture, Georges Rouault's fifty-eight *Miserere* etchings, Robert Arneson's nuclear dreams in acrylic and oil stick on paper, and Käthe Kollwitz's sculptures are all visual commentaries on the fact that the name of war is Cain: We desire to be like God, and we deny, not just that we know where our brother is, or that we are our brothers' and sisters' keepers, but that we even *have* a brother or sister.

There is something irresistible in the Erasmian view of war as the ultimate human crime, especially when coupled with Karl Barth's contention in *Church Dogmatics* that "it only needed the atom and the hydrogen bomb to complete the self-disclosure of war."[11] Anything less than a nuclear explosion we call simply "conventional war," as if it were all in a day's work. But it is instructive to dip back into history and remember that in its modern form deterrence was first introduced by the British in the 1930s, partially because the awful memories of World War I were fresh in English minds and partially because the development of bombers threatened to wreak even greater havoc on the cities of this planet. It is not easy to oppose nuclear weapons but not conventional warfare when one remembers the Battle of the Somme or the bombing of Dresden. Fifty-five million people died in World War II, only two hundred and fifty thousand of them from nuclear weapons. More than twenty-five million people have died in the hundred or so wars since 1945 (more than in all of World War I), not a single one of them from nuclear weapons. Tokyo witnessed many more deaths from one fire raid than Hiroshima did from the A-bomb. One doubts God saw any difference in the smoke drifting through the sky over the burning bodies at Auschwitz and at Hiroshima. One wonders whether God's eyes have dried even yet.

Given the incredibly destructive qualities of conventional weapons, there seems little moral progress by humanity toward a world made safe for "conventional" war. This is why discussions of nuclear war which give overwhelming attention to "nuclear" and little to "war" are cause for concern. We need to be careful not to generate false hope by focusing on the elimination of nuclear weapons, when technological advances are fast making conventional weapons almost as dangerous. In fact, miniaturized nuclear weapons have almost eliminated the firebreak between conventional and nuclear weapons.

Solving the nuclear question does not solve our problems and may not even solve our hardest problem. For even if we rid ourselves of all nuclear weapons, we would still have the war problem. Perhaps the most memorized lines during the Spanish Civil War came from a poem by Stephen Spender that first appeared in the *New Statesman* in May 1937. Why these words alone are not sufficient to stop all fighting is a mystery.

> The guns spell money's ultimate reason
> In letters of lead on the Spring hillside.
> But the boy lying dead under the olive trees
> Was too young and too silly
> To have been notable to their important eye.
> He was a better target for a kiss.[12]

Our goal must be not just to prevent nuclear war but to end all war. But the war problem is grievously and dangerously exacerbated because we no longer merely think in terms of war; we now think in nuclear terms, which has introduced, along with modern technology, a whole new way of thinking about war.

Former Secretary of State Alexander Haig sat before the Senate Armed Forces Committee one afternoon and uttered an unforgettable sentence: "There are worse things in the world than nuclear war." Can there be worse things in this world than atomic, biological, and chemical war? Both our sanity and our survival depend on unblinkered thinking about this question. I have come to the conclusion that the answer is no, which makes me a relative or what some call a "just-war" pacifist, or a "nuclear" pacifist. The reason is that nuclear war is not war. Neither is it suicide.[13] Nor is it genocide.[14] Rather, it is "terracide" and "omnicide." It is death of earth and death of birth, or what some German scholars are calling *Entschöpfung,* which literally translates as "discreation." As the United Methodist bishops have pointed out in their marvelously titled *In Defense of Creation,* the classic formulation of war as a continuation of politics by other means is inapplicable to thermonuclear war. Like pregnancy, there's no such thing as a little war. We are accustomed to thinking of modern warfare as different from pre-nuclear warfare merely in degree: We can expect millions or even billions of deaths in a nuclear war, although the Federal Emergency Management Agency (FEMA) boasts that it can hold down casualties to forty-five million if Americans will only do this:

> Take the time you need to pack.
> Prepare your home as if you were leaving for a vacation.
> Draw your curtains and drapes.
> Take along all perishables.
> Take a portable toilet with you.
> 15 double bed sheets should be in each shelter.
> Bring your credit cards.[15]

But modern war is different from pre-nuclear warfare not just in degree but in kind. We are talking about an entirely new reality and taking a moral quantum leap when we shift from pre-nuclear weapons to the technological elixir of atomic, biological, and chemical weapons. "The nuclear age confronts us," Helmut Thielicke writes, "with change not merely in the form, but in the very nature of war."[16] The bomb is less a weapon of war than a weapon of terracide.

Lamech, descendant of Cain, was the first figure in biblical history to present the problem of the appropriate use of force.

> Adah and Zillah, hear my voice,
> wives of Lamech, listen to what I say:
> I killed a man for wounding me,
> a boy for striking me.
> Sevenfold vengeance for Cain,
> but seventy-sevenfold for Lamech.
> (Genesis 4:23 NJB)

It is one thing to be a proponent of massive retaliation, or to wield swords against warriors that "utterly destroy" (I Samuel 15:3 RSV). There is a world of difference, however, and more than a new and greater degree of massiveness in employing modern technological arsenals of terracide to take revenge and to resolve conflicts and disputes.

In the science fiction novel *Starship Troopers* (1959), Robert A. Heinlein graphically makes this point. A sergeant responds to a new recruit's question about why we should send our boys to die in hand-to-hand combat when we have these planet-busting bombs to work for us, by saying, "[Do you] spank a baby with an ax?" Paul says there are certain things so awful they should not even be mentioned. In fact, usage of the word "war" in the same sentence with the word "nuclear" ought to be banned. "Nuclear war" is a lie. One scholar concludes that because "nuclear war" involves people who neither claim the ideologies of the contestants nor consent to the use of their bodies, it conforms more to the model of torture than to that of conventional war.[17]

Simply for the sake of argument, let us make the immoral concession that the defense of liberty may require that just-war restraints be abrogated. Conventional wars end in victory or defeat. Granted, war has never had any real victors. The meaning of victory is, well, somewhat elliptical. If you look at the current economic situation in light of World War II, victory means you do not get to build new factories as do the nations you defeated. This allows their modernized factories (which you helped rebuild) to overtake your economy. The only true victory, in the aftermath of a nuclear holocaust, is victory for rats and cockroaches—rats because they always survive, cockroaches because they are resistant to radiation. The widely quoted line, "The turtles that are left will wear human-neck sweaters," is more prophecy than sick joke.

Let us make one final, strenuous effort to be agreeable. For the sake of argument and in the absence of hard empirical evidence to the contrary, let us assume that Planet Earth will not be obliterated or rendered uninhabitable by a nuclear winter. Let us momentarily ponder the attitude of the Civil Defense Preparedness Agency's pamphlet *Protection in the Nuclear Age* (1977), which portrays nuclear war as a two-week hiatus from normalcy, an abbreviated lacuna of lunacy. To be sure, we need not go as berserk in our thinking as the Defense Department ranking official for research on nuclear war, who announced in 1981 that "if there are enough shovels to go around, everybody's going to make it." All that needs to be done in the event of a nuclear alert is for each one of us to dig a hole three feet deep, crawl in, cover it somehow, and wait. "It's the dirt that does it."[18] But let us admit that those who say that a very limited nuclear exchange is possible are right. Let us concede that only forty to fifty million Americans and fifty to sixty million Russians (20 percent of whom, by the way, are said to be Jews and Christians) will be wiped out. What kind of victory will survivors enjoy? What kind of liberty will victory bring? What will the liberty be like that has been bought with the price of one hundred million lives?

Surely trauma stirs ahead for them in the shadows. The staggering strains on sanity and on social order stretch the boundaries of the imagination. We shiver upon learning from Saturninus that the streets of ancient Rome were such that a dog might pick up a human hand and bring it into the house. The *hibakusha* ("explosion-afflicted" survivors of Hiroshima and Nagasaki) only begin to reveal how much worse it would be in the aftermath of a nuclear holocaust. One can only guess at the psychological shock and terror of those remaining. They would be a people suspicious of any authority; a people hating all governments; a people feeling guilty to be alive; a people suspicious and fearful of one another, the bonds of community irreparably broken; a people despairing of the future; a people stripped of prior standards of living and morality by the brutish conditions under which they would be forced to live. Since the radiation effect of nuclear devastation would be, for Planet Earth, a death that never dies, imagine the centuries-long horror that would haunt the couples of the future, who would have to face the possibility of giving birth to genetically damaged children.[19] Is this a victory for liberty?

It seems so obvious that an ABC war would lead not to the creation of a free society, but to the cremation of a free society. Can there be such a thing as a war for liberty when liberty is its prime casualty? Can there be such a thing as a war for justice and truth when justice and truth become meaningless in the aftermath? What conceivable issue could be solved, or cultural identity preserved, by nuclear conflagration? Dylan Thomas's elegiac poem, "A Refusal to Mourn the Death by Fire, of a Child in London," has a strange last line: "After the first death, there is no other."[20]

The first nuclear exchange will redefine all terms and usher in a new language which does not distinguish between victory and defeat, winners and losers, right and wrong. Nuclear war empties every word and every value of meaning. In that period of seven minutes or seven days, the alphabet will have been invented anew.

Just before Patrick Henry's concluding sentence, he said, "Is life so dear, or peace so sweet, as to be purchased at the price of chains and slavery?" A nuclear world reverses these sentiments. The price of life and peace, when purchased by nuclear armaments, is chains, slavery, and death.

Patrick Henry prefaced the above famous phrase with words that are seldom quoted: *"I know not what course others may take;* but as for me, give me liberty or give me death." This is the fundamental seam in the logic of nuclear defense that my nightmare forced me to confront: "I know not what course others may take; but as for me . . ." In other words, Henry's statement was a very personal testament spoken by a man who had made his choice, was ready to face the consequences, and was urging others to come to a similar decision. In a nuclear society, however, persons are denied the right to make this decision. I have the right to sacrifice my life for a principle. I do not have the right to sacrifice your life for my principles. Whereas soldiers give up their rights to life and liberty, citizens do not. Even if one acquiesces to a radical reading of the Constitution, giving one person the right to decide for me whether I get liberty or death, the Constitution clearly does not give anyone the right to decide whether my children (and their children) get liberty or death.

Who gives an American president the right to decide whether Canadians or Mexicans get liberty or death? Is this not to raise one person—or one computer—to the level of idolatry? The question of the nature of governmental authority poses the most critical issue of political science in our day, especially when our definition of liberty seems perilously close to our definition of capitalism. Restraints on the limits of governance have not kept pace with the developments of technology. International law also is virtually blind to terracidal warfare. Adam Roberts has shown that "in the forty years since 1945 there have been ten new international agreements on the laws of war, totalling perhaps 100,000 words, yet the words 'nuclear weapons' do not occur once in them."[21]

Anyone who raises such questions today risks being branded with the epithet first spoken by Bertrand Russell, "Better red than dead." There is that ubiquitous question, What about a Russian invasion of the U.S.? Well, what about it? I deeply believe in democratic values and democratic institutions. The love of freedom and liberty glows brightly in my soul. My response would probably be involvement in a resistance movement, depending on what shape that took. I may be willing to say, "Give me liberty or give me death." Because of the nature of a specific community, I may even be willing to say, "Give you liberty or give you death." But I am not willing to say, "Give our children liberty or give them death," or "Give the future liberty or give the future death." I am not willing to deprive our children of what Peter Porter, in a moving poem, calls the "story which should have happened."[22]

E. P. Thompson warned recently that "nothing less than a worldwide spiritual revulsion against the Satanic kingdom would give us any chance of bringing the military riders down."[23] Very early on Albert Einstein issued a similar challenge: "Unless the cause of peace based on law gathers behind it the force and zeal of a religion, it hardly can hope to succeed. Those to whom the moral teaching of the human race is entrusted surely have a great duty and a great opportunity."[24] Such summons for people of faith to get their act together are as acute as they are awkward. For while we as Christians and Jews have some singular contributions to make to the discussion, we have one disadvantage—we cause people to think. Alexander Haig's contention that there are "some things worse than nuclear war," for example, raises the sobering question of what are the worst things in the world. Social ethicist Richard J. Mouw tells the story of one of his teachers defending pacifism before a class of skeptical students. When one of the students unleashed the customary criticism that usually quells debate—the pacifist stigma of issuing an open invitation for Russia to march in and take over the country—the professor replied, "That is not the worst thing that could happen to me. . . . The worst thing that could happen to me would be for the Russians to separate me from the love of God which is in Jesus Christ. But I know they can't do that."[25] Tyranny is not the worst thing that could happen to us, as precious as freedom is. The worst thing in the world is life without faith, hope, and love in our hearts. As Jews and Christians first and patriots second, we possess the peace that passes the understanding of all races, all classes, all nations.

Paul found liberty locked up in prison. What is more, while incarcerated Paul reasoned that his being jailed actually transpired for the good of the gospel. His unwilling presence among the Roman troops allowed him to testify in word and deed to an otherwise inaccessible audience. If Russia were to imprison American Christians and Jews, might not the same thing happen? Could not the odd God of Romans 9–11 work today in such mysterious ways?

One contribution Christians and Jews can make to the overhaul in our thinking about nuclear destruction is to address the question of what makes a nation strong. Our militarized mind-set, the ideology of peace through power, which has led to our equation of a *Pax Americana* with a *Pax Atomica,* is relatively recent in American history. In Patrick Henry's speech he admitted that the colonies were, in the minds of many, weak and probably "unable to cope with so

36

formidable an adversary," but "the battle, sir, is not to the strong alone; it is to the vigilant, the active, the brave." For too long we have been led to believe that the battle is to the strong alone, that the basic strength of a nation is measured in missiles, megatons, and might. Peace, freedom, liberty, and justice come more from weaponry than from divinity, we have been told, as we put our national security in the hands of the right of force more than the force of right. No argument from me will attend the cry for a strong national defense. Swans, like nations, keep their distance from one another. Disagreement comes with the current understanding of what constitutes strong national defense. National security is diminished, not enhanced, by nuclear weaponry. We are less secure today with over twenty thousand nuclear weapons than we were right after World War II with only two nuclear weapons. America is inadequately defended by nuclear weaponry.

When Jesus said, "Love your enemies" (Matthew 5:44), he meant it. Love is stronger than any atomic "pestilence that stalks in darkness" or "destruction that wastes at noonday" (Psalm 91:6 RSV). W. H. Auden wrote, as World War II was breaking out, that "we must love one another or die."[26] Our foreign policy is based on the belief that we must "outnuke" one another or die. The most powerful, the most invincible, the strongest national defense we can have is spiritual, not material; it is a matter of will, not weaponry. If it took only three little stones for David to slay Goliath, why do we require billions?

The collective resolve and spirit of the people has been our strongest defense in the past, which is why America was celebrated as the land of the future. Today we are weakest in the realm of the spiritual, which is why America appears more and more to have become merely the land with a promising past. And the weaker we become in spirit, the harder we try to appear strong in might. The stronger the will and spirit, the less need there is to show strength in weapons and speech. If we were as secure as we say we are, our military establishment would be trained at a peace academy rather than a war college,[27] the chief purpose of our armed forces would be not to "win wars" but to "avert wars,"[28] our leaders would be talking to us in "peacespeak," not "nukespeak," and our people would be up to their necks not funding the rat race or the arms race but a peace race, a food race, and a health race.

The United States and the Soviet Union are moral equivalents of the pre-repentant Zacchaeus, in our world. As it is now, through the manufacturing and marketing of nuclear weapons of destruction, these two alleged "superpowers" are creating one of the most serious mental health problems in history—a no-hope life. They are also guilty of some of the gravest human rights violations in the world—one of which is the fundamental right to a human destiny. A no-hope life is the acid rain of the spirit. A no-life hope is the nuclear rain of the mind. America opened Pandora's box on August 6, 1945. America has a special obligation to close it.

The best of the Jewish-Christian tradition has said that violence is not the most effective form of power. Paul said simply, "For when I am weak, then I am strong" (II Corinthians 12:10). The most powerful forces in the world are not physical but spiritual. It is time we become serious about our faith and stop playing around. Either there is a God or there isn't a God. If there is a God, then God is not one word among many words. It is time not only to believe in God. It is time to believe God.

And stop hobbling. "How long . . . do you mean to hobble first on one leg then on the other?" Elijah thundered to the Hebrew throngs on Mount Carmel. "If Yahweh is God, follow him; if Baal, follow him" (I Kings 18:21 NJB). It is time to believe God, to follow God. It is time to hear Jesus say, "No more of this!" (Luke 22:51).

CHAPTER 2

The Hunter
and the Shepherd

The only people on earth who do not see Christ and his
teachings as nonviolent are Christians.
—Mohandas Gandhi

Before people of faith can speak to the world a message of
peace, we first have to learn a little Hebrew. The blessing
narrative of Genesis 27:1-46 picks up the dramatic story of
Jacob and Esau's rivalry, first introduced in the birthright
narrative of 25:27-34. Isaac is now an old man. His eyes have
deteriorated to the point where he is legally blind. According
to rabbinic tradition, when Isaac lay bound on the altar, about
to be sacrificed by his father, the angels wept tears that fell
upon his eyes and progressively weakened his sight.

The customary reading of this passage accents the
deception of Jacob and Rebekah, or what Jacob did to his
father. There is a rabbinic tradition, however, that says the
fullest meaning of the story is to be found not in what Jacob
did to his father, but in what Jacob did to himself. If that is the
case, the most significant verse in the whole story may be
verse 32, the one customarily overlooked: "His father Isaac
said, 'Who are you?' He said, 'I am Esau, your elder son.'
Then Isaac became greatly agitated." Isaac is presented as
being "greatly agitated" (or "incensed," as *The New English
Bible* has it in the footnotes). But the Hebrew word denotes
both strong emotion and physical expression. Some Hebrew
translations render it "trembled violently."

Can you imagine a scene more filled with pathos and poignancy than this one between Isaac and Esau—the father helpless and trembling, the son weeping bitterly? Only one other time did Isaac tremble so violently, and that was when his father Abraham bound him to the altar and raised the knife to slay him. But this fright and shaking was even greater than before. Isaac trembled so violently, the midrash tells us, not because his son had deceived him, but because his son who was set apart to be a shepherd, called by God to be a herdsman, had put on the clothing of a hunter. When Isaac realized what Jacob had done to himself, how he had violated God's ambition for him, which was to tend flocks, not stalk game, how he had compromised the integrity of his identity by putting on hunting gear rather than taking up the staff, he trembled and cried out for Jacob: "What have you done? Not to me. Not to your brother Esau. What have you done to you?"

God is trembling violently right now. For God's church, born a Jacob, perpetually becomes an Esau. Yahweh told Pharaoh in Exodus 8:23, "I will make a distinction between my people and yours." God's people, destined to live as shepherds, too often prefer to look like Pharaoh's people, wearing the clothing and equipment of soldiers. The church in "drag" is not a pretty sight. Look at many of our conferences (United Methodist), conventions (Baptist), and presbyteries (Presbyterian). We have become so political that Republicans and Democrats could learn something from us. My eight-year-old son Justin challenges me constantly to play the game of "Ewoks," and I routinely get trounced. These sessions are constant reminders of street wisdom: "Never take someone on when they're playing their own game." The church needs to be very careful about its adoption of political paradigms and initiatives. The political game was not set up with the church in mind, and politically oriented efforts to combat evil and "organize to beat the devil" give us the appearance, and often have the same consequence, of fighting the devil with fire. Like Dante's use of Lucifer's leg to escape the Inferno, it is one thing to use political structures to move the world beyond the conundrums that our politics have generated. It is another thing to hire the devil to fight the devil. Harry Emerson Fosdick's most powerful pacifist sermon put the issue in its starkest form: "Can Satan Cast Out Satan?"[1] Can we beat evil at its own game? Is it true, in the words of that old saying, that "only the Devil can save us now, and you ask for saints"?

Or look at the spirit of many of our churches. A cartoon in *The New Yorker* shows Moses having parted the waters of the Red Sea and the Israelites moving through the passage. Moses, appearing very irritated, is saying to the man next to him: "Of course it's damp underfoot. That strikes me as a very petty complaint to be making at a time like this." The issue is not merely complaint-sogged congregations, or how few of us really want to get our feet wet in our faith, but how few of us treat each other as if we were brothers and sisters in the faith. There is a saying attributed to Abbot Hyperechius, a sixth-century monastic: "It is better to eat flesh and to drink wine than to eat the flesh of the brethren by backbiting them." How many church members (so the joke goes) have come to church in one cab and left in two? How many Christians and Jews can claim with Martin Luther King, Jr., that they "avoid not only external physical violence but also internal violence of spirit."[2] How many churches have members who behave like cats in a sack, clawing and scratching each other? How many clergy savage each other mercilessly? The great fundamentalist leader J. Frank Norris had a Southern Baptist rival who in his earlier years had accidentally run over and killed a child. On each anniversary of the boy's death, Norris is said to have arranged for someone to slip a message into the pulpit that Sunday wishing him a happy anniversary. The church boasts a shameful record of violence in its own life and ethos.

History is violent, and the church has been involved in that violence to a frightful degree. Ugly outcroppings of witch hunts and heresy hunts, holy wars and holy inquisitions, disfigure the history of the church. The bloodcurdling history of wars reveals that the majority were fought over religion; even those that weren't, the church has blessed. Edward Westermarck's *The Origin and Development of the Moral Ideal* concludes, "It would be impossible to find a single instance of a war waged by a Protestant country, from any motive, to which the bulk of its clergy have not given their sanction and support."[3]

The Bible has been credited with sustaining men in battle more than any other book, its only competition being the *Encheiridion of Epictetus* (ca. A.D. 55–135). Mark Twain, whose satiric *The War Prayer* (1923) is a minor classic of antiwar literature, liked to say that religion is pretty dangerous stuff if you get it wrong. We need go no further than the crucifixion of Jesus to see how wrong we can get it. It was the religious establishment, not the world, that crucified Jesus. If you expect the devil to have horns, you'll never see him. More often than not, the devil wears a halo. In the words of Reinhold Niebuhr, "The church can be the anti-Christ; and when it denies that possibility, it is the anti-Christ."[4] The church can become, in Tennyson's phrase, "procuress to the Lords of hell" as well as to the Lord of the Dance.

The church has been much too ready to hear the voices of Vulcan and Mars and to warmonger with Wotan by blessing cannons, bullets, and bombs. As Harvard humorist, songwriter, and mathematician Tom Lehrer put it in "Who's Next?"

> "The Lord's our shepherd," says the psalm.
> But, just in case, we better get a bomb.

Our children no longer send in fifteen cents and one Kix cereal box top, as over one million of them did in 1946, in return for an "Atomic Bomb Ring" offered by General Mills Corporation. But they collect "Garbage Pail Kids" stickers, contemporary alternatives to baseball cards bearing grotesque, perverse pictures of children involved in violence, with names like "Gored Gordon," "Shorn Sean," "Trashed Tracy," "Nailed Neil," "Deadly Dudley," "Rock E. Horror," "Decapitated Hedy," and "Dyin' Dinah." The most popular one is "Adam Bomb," which shows a seated child pushing a red button with his thumb, a blood-red mushroom cloud popping out of his exploding head.

Images of violence and horror work hard to establish that God is, as Woody Allen has instructed us, "an underachiever." An old New England cemetery reveals that felling human beings with an ax and "falling asleep in the arms of Jesus" were not mutually exclusive. An inscription on a gravestone reads:

> He killed eighty Indians.
> He wanted to live to kill one hundred,
> but he was prevented, because
> he fell asleep in the arms of Jesus.

Nazi guards at crematoriums proclaimed faith in God on Sunday and on Monday complained about their working conditions, particularly the discomfort of the noxious odor of the excrement expelled by their dying victims. Christians applauding the neutron bomb as a "clean bomb" are heralding one of the most unclean things imaginable—an instrument that kills people but leaves buildings standing. Christians at a nuclear supply firm in West Germany can be heard justifying from the Bible their working for a company with the name NUKEM. Christians in America virtually have one finger on the nuclear bomb and the other finger in the Bible.

These metaphors and images are more than mere euphemisms of death. They are symbols of the church's relaxed conscience about war and the way in which Mars still rules the mind of the church. Soul-sucking forces have twisted and tortured the church's mind out of its true shape. If something is not done quickly, the time is fast approaching when the church will be like a band of elastic that has been so stretched and pulled that it can never return to its original and true form. When the band passes beyond that certain point, one of two things happens: The mind of the church becomes limp and lifeless, or it snaps.

The original and true form of the church is as different as the church of our dreams and the church of our waking hours. There is an incredible contrast between the primitive pacifism of the age of the martyrs and the militarism of today. In fact, the church's switch from wearing the clothes of Jacob to the clothes of Esau is one of the most remarkable about-faces in history. I do not want to suggest that Christianity is alone in its ecclesiastical transvestism; all the major religions of the world have accommodated themselves to the needs and climates of their societies and nations. It is one thing to be a lover of peace when someone else has all the arms and all the numbers. It is another thing to be a pacifist when we are in power and are the majority.

I also do not want to suggest that we would not have accepted Constantine's offer if we had been the early church. After three centuries of having been food for lions and fuel for streetlamps (Nero tied Christians to stakes, doused them with oil, and lit them to provide light for his parties), I doubt we would have resisted any more successfully than the early church Constantine's temptation, when he raised the cross above his troops. But I do want us to remember that the early church found it significant that the last miracle Jesus performed was the healing of a wound inflicted by one of his own disciples' weapons. "In disarming Peter," Tertullian said, "Christ unbelted every soldier."[5] The early church by and large refused military service and condoned non-Christian participation in warfare only when there was "humane" fighting.

To be sure, in the history of the Christian church just-war theory was not simply a youthful fit which became a lifelong habit. It was employed from the very beginning as an extension of the Old Testament ethic of the just use of force. The early church's position on war and the military had great color and complexity; it was much less easy and uniform than Roland H. Bainton asserted in his widely quoted *Christian Attitudes Toward War and Peace*.[6] Their position had more to do with opposition to pagan exercises; to idolatrous oaths, clothing, and ceremonies; and to the church's general "Christ-against-culture" posture, than with a sixties-style pure pacifism.[7] The theoretical pacifism of the early church was as much shaped by social and political forces as the "just warriors" were after Constantine.

Yet in spite of evidence that some early Christians in the Cornelius tradition were involved in the military (which was as much the equivalent of today's police force as an army), at least after A.D. 170, and that the church fathers did not deny a nation's right to go to war to protect its citizens,[8] the overwhelming witness of the early church was one of opposition to Christian complicity in warfare. "God designed iron for tilling, not for killing," Cyprian exclaimed. No amount of threat or torture would budge him from this faith. In his first trial in A.D. 257, the proconsul gave him an opportunity to change his mind and recant. Cyprian replied, "A good mind, which knows God, it is not possible to change."[9] Similarly, Maximilianus of Numidia was called up for military service at age twenty-one because he was the son of a Roman army veteran. He refused to serve, even when some Christians had already begun serving, saying: "Non possum militare, non possum malefacere—Christianus sum" ("I cannot serve as a soldier, I cannot do evil; I am a Christian").[10] Maximilianus was executed in A.D. 295, one of the first recorded instances of religious conscientious objection to military service.

It is one thing to accept war as an irrepressible part of the life of other thrones and dominions; it is another thing to approve and legitimate war as a part of the life of the church. What led the church to change its mind and legitimate warfare, moving it from a no-war mentality to a just-war and even a holy-war position, where our "feet are swift to shed blood" (Romans 3:15 RSV), was Constantine's adoption of Cicero's theory of just wars, for use in a Christianized Roman Empire. Revised successively by Augustine, Gregory, and Bernard, then codified by Aquinas, the theory of the just war developed most fully between the ninth and thirteenth centuries. Just-war doctrines were retained by the Reformers, given classic shape by Francisco de Vitoria and Francisco Suárez in the sixteenth century, then given creedal authority in the seventeenth century.[11] Today the notion of justified violence rules the thinking of both church and state, with ever-expanding definitions of what is "justified." While Henry Kissinger is astute in his suspicion that pacifism is on the rise in the world today because ordinary people can no longer find sensible alternative choices, the no-war tradition has a long way to go before it even begins to draw near to the early church, where the burden of proof was on the believer to demonstrate why he or she was not a pacifist.

William Howard Taft's great-granddaughter was asked to write her autobiography in the third grade. This is what she wrote: "My great-grandfather was president of the U.S., my grandfather was a U.S. senator, my father was an ambassador, and I am a Brownie." God meant the church to be a great force for peace in our world. The church carries, like that third-grader, the genetics of greatness. What is keeping the church from growing into greatness for peace? Two things.

Shortly after I moved to Ohio, I was stopped at a random roadblock by the Ohio State Highway Patrol. I drove away with a ticket for having a "bad body" and a "weak horn." A "bad body"—the nature of the community—and a "weak horn"—the power of proclamation—were two major concerns Rebekah and Isaac respectively had about Jacob.

In Genesis 27:46 Rebekah warns Jacob about marrying out of the tribe and tradition. "I am weary to death of Hittite women" like the ones Esau married, she laments. Integration with alien values and beliefs is destructive of community. It works against building a healthy and vital community life. The body of Christ should be a shalom community, a messianic community where human relationships are reordered and restructured, where people are more important than property, cooperation more valued than competition, self-sacrifice more appealed to than self-interest, and where people are living nonviolent ways of life. The word "shalom" occurs over 350 times in the Old Testament. Not *once* does "shalom" refer to an internal peace or an inner attitude. Shalom is a communal concept; Shalom is God's vision for the church. The difference between the Old Testament and the New Testament concept of shalom is that in the New Testament shalom becomes incarnate in the church, the body of Christ, or in what are best called koinonia communities ("kingdom" or "Christbody" communities). It is these body-neglecting (if not at times body-hating) communities that are in such bad shape. And if the body is neglected, it soon makes its presence felt.

All of us like to think of the church as the world's peace center, the one place in the world where we are able to preserve some space for peace. The great confusion over the meaning of this word "peace" has serious consequences for the church's mission of reproducing shalom communities. Jesus anticipated our confusion, for he chose his words very carefully when he told his disciples in John 14:27 (RSV), "My peace I give to you." And then, as if to avoid any further misunderstanding, he continued, "Not as the world gives, give I unto you."

Christ did not come to give peace as the world gives peace, but he realized that the world does give a kind of peace. When the ancient Greeks spoke of peace, as they did often, they had in mind the goddess of peace, Irene (from which we get our word "irenic"). But it is interesting that in pictures and statuary Irene is often accompanied by a little boy. The boy is the child Pluto, who represented prosperity, riches, and wealth. That is what the Greeks regarded as peace—making money, growing rich, achieving security. And money does bring a kind of peace. Ask those who don't have any. But Christ came to declare war on the peace of Pluto.

The ancient Romans also talked a lot about peace and personalized it in the goddess Pax. Around her head she wore a laurel wreath, the emblem of worldly honor and fame. That is what the Romans regarded as peace—success and power and fame. And there is a kind of peace that comes from success and fame and power. Ask those who don't have any. But Christ came to declare war on the peace of Pax.

The dominant social philosophy of our day is Greco-Roman—one of money and might. Personal power and economic realities are what really count, we think, and homage to Pluto and Pax have all too prominent a place in the body of Christ. The reason why some churches seem lifeless, almost as if the Holy Spirit had inhaled, is because they are dead, and we helped kill them with our greater interest in keeping them loyal to an organization than alive for Christ. The reason why some of our church conferences and assemblies are so marred by political intrigue and jockeying for position is that we have been more seduced by the love of power than by the power of love. We have forgotten that something can be procedurally correct and theologically wrong. The reason why the church is often its own worst enemy in trying to convince people to give peace a chance is that we are projecting an image when we should be reflecting an image—the image of Christ. The reason some Christians are as spiritually exciting as soggy potato chips is that we have been more concerned with keeping an organization going by keeping everyone busy than with filling the vacuum of emptiness inside people's lives.

The reason why the history of some of our congregations sounds like a chapter out of the book of Judges is that we gave them a paint job when what they really needed was a house cleaning. We let them forget that peace comes through atonement, not attainment. In the comic strip "Kudzu," Preacher Will B. Dunn goes into the pulpit and says to the congregation: "Brothers and Sisters, today I want to give you a test—a spiritual test. The test will measure your level of spiritual development as a congregation. Ready! First question! Complete the sentence: Whosoever will strike you on your first cheek . . . " Immediately, cries arise from the congregation: "String him up!" "Waste him!" Preacher Dunn responds, "I may be forced to grade this one on a curve."

If Rebekah was consumed by the dangers of a "bad body," Isaac registered his caution about a "weak horn." "The voice is Jacob's voice," Isaac observed in 27:22, "but the hands are the hands of Esau." Is the church putting more trust and confidence in the overpowering hands of Esau than in the empowering voice of Jacob? The Psalmist says, "Some trust in chariots, and some in horses, but we trust in the name of the Lord our God" (Psalm 20:7 NIV). If the church really believed that the power of Jacob's voice is greater than the might of Esau's hand . . . If the church really believed that the hands of Esau, skilled as they are in death and stained with the blood of conquest, are no match for the voice of Jacob. . . If the church really believed, in the words of Zechariah 4:6 (RSV) " 'Not by might, nor by power, but by my spirit,' says the Lord of Hosts" . . .

If the church really believed all this, then we could go on

and recite the next verse: "What are you, O great mountain? Before Zerubbabel you shall become a plain" (Zechariah 4:7 RSV). As long as the voice of Jacob can be heard, the ghastly empire of evil quakes. And by the voice of Jacob I mean sure-fire, hell-fire preaching of the Word of God, which has molded the preacher as surely as God's spoken word took hold of Isaiah and Jeremiah, Ezekiel and Hosea, as surely as Christ's spoken word mesmerized Matthew and Mary Magdalene, and spellbound Simon Peter and the Samaritan woman.

But the hands of Esau look so much more mighty and inviting. So we con our consciences into hitching our hopes to horses, chariots, cruise missles, and backfire bombers. We try to keep the peace by sticking to our guns. Why was King David condemned for what seemed a harmless exercise, taking a census and numbering the people? Because that act was an expression of David's pride in the hands of Esau—the size of the nation—rather than in the voice of Jacob—the power of God through thoughts that breathe and words that burn. In the first century B.C., the famous inventor and mathematician Archimedes uttered these famous words about the lever: "Give me where to stand, and I will move the earth." The writer Joseph Conrad updated that statement: "Don't speak to me of Archimedes' lever. Just give me the right *word,* and I will move the world." The church holds that right word. And the word is "Christ."

Why are we so afraid of our powers? Why has the church not yet found its voice? Why are we reluctant to say this word? Why is the church's domain still the empire of Esau, not Jacob? The "Scheherazade Syndrome" goes a long way in explaining the ascendancy of Esau's descendents in the church. The frame story for *The Arabian Nights* is the tale of the heroine Scheherazade, the daughter of the Grand Vizier who marries the Sultan Shahriar after he has vowed to marry a new wife every day and kill each bride the following morning. Scheherazade wields the weapon of entertainment—she tells a new tale to her husband every night and refuses to finish it until the next—to avoid her fate and save the lives of innumerable future wives. Journalists use the phrase "Scheherazade Syndrome" to describe how the readers of a paper form a kind of collective sultan who communicates the unspoken message: "If you bore me, you die." In other words, we are caught in the grip of fear—fear of losing our jobs, fear of the size of the obstacles that stand in the path to peace.

There is an old story about the driver of a transport truck hauling new automobiles to a dealership. While driving across a stretch of very foggy valley road, the trucker stopped and turned on the headlights of the car above the cab, to give additional light on the road. As the truck proceeded down the highway, two sets of headlights shining, it met an oncoming car. The car swerved into a roadside field and sank into the mud. The driver stopped the truck, ran out to the car, and said, "What happened to you?" The other driver said, "I took one look at that thing coming at me down the highway and figured that if it was as wide as it was high, I could never get around it!" Life's problems seem like that. They are big, but fear's darkness even makes them bigger, so we're run off the road by our fears, and sometimes killed.

There is a fable that tells of an oriental monarch who met Pestilence on the road to Bagdad. The monarch asked, "What are you going to do there?" Pestilence replied, "I am going to kill five thousand." On the way back, the monarch met Pestilence again. "You liar," he thundered, "you killed twenty-five thousand." "Oh, no," said Pestilence, "I killed five thousand. It was fear that killed the rest." Fear kills, literally. Most drowning victims do not die of asphyxiation. Autopsies reveal that there is not enough water in their lungs to drown them. They die before they drown, from fear. Many

51

snakebite victims do not die from the poisonous venom surging through their veins. Autopsies show that there is not enough poison in their bodies to kill them. They die instead from fear.

Fear of the bomb can be more dangerous than the bomb itself, just as the fear of the Soviet Union is more dangerous than the Soviet Union itself. Throughout American history, the chilling winds of nativist fears have blown across the back of our necks. In the nineteenth century, fear targeted the Roman Catholics, or as they were then called, the Roman Ruin. Then came the Black Danger. Then the Red Revolution. Then the Yellow Peril. Then the Red Threat. Then the Pink menace. And now there is a return to the well-orchestrated Rhapsody-in-Red fear of the twenties and fifties. Billy Sunday claimed that if you turned the pot of hell upside down, you would find "Made in Germany" stamped on the bottom. Today many Christians expect to find "Made in Russia" stamped on the bottom. Studs Terkel comments on this widespread fear of communism and Russia: "At the moment, a great many of us live in our fifty-first state, Catatonia. It is far more populous than California, New York, Pennsylvania, Ohio, Illinois, and Michigan put together.[12]

The story is told about a temperance speaker who announced from the pulpit that he was going to speak on the evils of liquor, and that he was full of his subject. That is exactly what has happened to the United States and the Soviet Union, in their relationship to each other. They are two "bumbling giants" (Richard Barnet), each "armed camps" (E. P. Thompson), both hardened "materialists" (Dale Vree), ideological look-alikes (the Russians declaim against American "imperialism," the Americans declaim against Russian "totalitarianism")—mirror images of each other, each being consumed by the evil they oppose.[13] You can be destroyed by evil as much through hating it as loving it.

Even peacemakers can be so filled with hatred of war that they run the risk of becoming, like Captain Ahab in *Moby Dick*, exactly like what they oppose. Abraham Lincoln warned the abolitionists not to be so self-righteous that they started looking and acting like slaveholders. All "new abolitionists" need a similar warning.

This is not to suggest that the United States and the Soviet Union are moral equivalents, "as if a man fled from a lion and a bear met him" (Amos 5:19 RSV). The U.S. and the U.S.S.R are not the Tweedledum and Tweedledee of superpowers. The moral difference between them is much larger than the difference in their initials. The Russian bear is like any bear: It can get you by chasing you down, but it can get you even more quickly by hugging you to death. Russian repression and Gulag brutality are frightening. Soviet officials contend for the minds and hearts of their people by putting a bullet through either or both. Official Soviet atheism is genuinely chilling. One Soviet poster shows the pregnant Virgin Mary looking at a billboard advertising a film on abortion. In the caption she exclaims, "Oh, why didn't I know that before!"[14]

But Russia also is being strangled by the grip of fear. If Canada and Mexico were well armed and dangerous, Americans might understand a little better the situation facing the Soviets. Furthermore, is it unfair to say that more than a measure of *obscenity* can be found in the world's first atom bomb being named "Trinity" or in the distorted confusion of the motto of many modern armies, "Peace is our profession"? Does not a portion of *profanity* reside in the prayer used at the "christening" of a submarine: "God bless this submarine, may it be an instrument of peace"? Is not *blasphemy* voiced when America's flashy new sports-weapon, the MX missile (you can always tell a sports model by the X in its title), is advertised as the "Peacekeeper"? Can one not detect *sacrilege* being committed when the town where all American nuclear bombs receive final assembly is impiously named Saint Francis, Texas? The inscription of the churchyard shrine in Saint Francis reads thus:

> O Blessed Lady, look down graciously upon the fields and pastures of this land. Make our homes sanctuaries of Christ as was thy home. Make our fields fertile and abundant in the harvest. Help us to more fully understand the dignity of our toil and the merit it acquires when offered through thee to thy Divine Son, Jesus Christ. Amen.[15]

If one wants to be afraid of "godless communism," then let's place some of those fears where they belong—in the West. There are more Christians attending church in Moscow than in London; more people go to church in the Soviet Union than in all of Western Europe.

One of the least understood aspects of modernization theory is the fact that all systems—and the arms race is a system—have a life of their own. If every single one of the world's leaders were replaced, but there were no attempts to unfasten the basic fears that bind us, absolutely nothing would change. The mission of the church is to attack the institutionalization of fear through the great news of the gospel. There is a Carillon Park in the city of Dayton, Ohio, that has on display some of the old vehicles, such as bicycles, cars, wagons, and trains, which were important to the development of the Miami Valley. One in particular catches my eye every time I go there. It is an early Miamisburg hand-drawn fire engine that took eighteen people to pull and pump. Emblazoned on its sides are these words for people in distress: "Fear Not We Come." This is how the world should see us: firefighters who douse the flames of fear with the water of God's Spirit.

What enables the church to break through the Scheherazade Syndrome and put out fears is the message of the mercy and long-suffering and "perfect love" of God. "Fear not," the Bible says, putting these two words together ninety-nine times. The first word spoken to his disciples by the resurrected Lord was "Shalom." Do not fear, all is well, everything is going to be all right (see Luke 24:36; John 20:19-22). "Be of good cheer" were the strange last words of Jesus' farewell discourse (John 16:33 RSV), given right after he had informed his followers about what to expect—hostility, hatred, and suffering. The Greek word *thaiseo* means "have courage" or "do not be afraid." "Be of good cheer! I have overcome the world."

"There is hope for your future, says the Lord" (Jeremiah 31:17 RSV). We fight only when we hope. Peacemakers must have great hope, because this world has so little of it. I am part of a generation whose parents built bomb shelters and whose teachers conducted duck-under-the-desk drills. It is now a sign of surreal optimism, if not implacable madness, to even think about bomb shelters. A rapid and rabid shift in our perspective on the future has taken place, until our children are now more optimistic about death than they are about life. The wheels of the divine chariot seem to be going backward rather than forward, and the question seems to be not if, but when, we shall reach the Omega point. Studies abound on the effect on people of television violence. Most focus on the fact that violence on television makes 2 percent of the population more violent. Most forget what kind of impact it has on the rest of the population: It makes the remaining 98 percent more frightened. And a frightened people are a fence-sitting people—a people who have difficulty making choices, a people who cannot get off the fence of fear, a more easily manipulated and controlled people, as well as a more hopeless people.

Even our educational institutions are contributing to the obliteration of traditional positive standards of reference and hope. A 1985 commencement address at the University of Chicago was titled "Extinction and Global Habitability." Its cheerful message was that virtually all species that have ever lived on earth are extinct. The speaker sent the graduates into the world with these ringing words:

> So, extinction has been about as common, in the long haul, as origination of species. And so, extinction of any given species is statistically almost inevitable. . . . The habitability of the earth is not an open-and-shut case and . . . it is also somewhat in the eye of the beholder. Finally I want to congratulate the degree candidates here today. You have completed programs at the best university in the world.[16]

We have done all the right things to bring our children to the point where suicide is the second leading cause of death among teenagers. The screams and scrambles of the materialists who have decided they might as well "go first class on the Titanic" are really nothing more than riots of the hopeless. In the words of Emily Dickinson, who I believe is the greatest poet America has produced:

> Will there really be a "Morning"?
> Is there such a thing as "Day"?
> Could I see it from the mountains
> If I were as tall as they?
>
> Has it feet like Water lilies?
> Has it feathers like a "Bird"
> Is it brought from famous countries
> Of which I have never heard?
>
> Oh, some Scholar! Oh, some Sailor!
> Oh, some Wise Man from the skies!
> Please tell a little Pilgrim
> Where the place called "Morning" lies![17]

"Morning has broken"—this is the special message Jesus gives to a skeptical world, to children being pushed to suicide by society. Hope is a rope that pulls people who are lost in the dark pit of self-absorption into the light of service. Like the hat the little boy threw over the high fence to make sure he would climb over it, throwing hope into the future ensures that we will enter that land and possess it. Before the church can present with conviction and power the biblical message of hope, the fears that choke its own faith and confidence must first be exorcized. Alas, the moving hands of the famous "minutes-to-midnight" doomsday clock tighten around the neck of the church as tightly as the world.

The church may need to learn a technique from Spanish matadors. Before a bullfight, they go off by themselves and perform one last ritual: they take a "leak of fear." It is only when the church has drained fear from its own system that it can offer the world the hope found in the song that film director Nicholas Meyers unwittingly used as background music for the opening and closing scenes of ABC's *The Day After:* the old gospel song "How Firm a Foundation." It includes these words:

> Fear not, I am with thee; O be not dismayed,
> For I am thy God, And will still give thee aid:
> I'll strengthen thee, help thee,
> and cause thee to stand,
> Upheld by my righteous omnipotent hand.

In an article acknowledging the twentieth anniversary of the Berlin Wall, *National Geographic* magazine ran a two-page aerial photograph of the wall.[18] The wall, which East Germany calls "an anti-fascist democratic protection barrier," is really a double wall. Between the walls there is a no-man's-land filled with all kinds of *débris* of destruction: upturned spikes, barbed wire, electric fences, trip alarms, watchdogs, floodlights, vehicle traps, etcetera. In this picture, however, one sees an abandoned church beween the double walls, surrounded by these instruments of hostility and death. It stands empty and unused. Ironically, the name of the church is "the Church of Reconciliation." Why the Soviets have allowed it to remain standing is a mystery. But it stands as a wonderful and powerful symbol of what the church is, and what the church might be.

In this world where Esau's hands are hard at work, the church must learn to be the voice of Jacob.

> The nations rage, the kingdoms totter;
>   he utters his voice, the earth melts.
> The Lord of hosts is with us,
>   the God of Jacob is our refuge.
>   (Psalm 46:6-7 RSV)

CHAPTER 3

The Day and Way of the Wolf

We must now face the fact that we are moving closer and closer to war, not only as a result of blind social forces but also as the result of our own decisions and our own choice. The brutal reality is that, when all is said and done, we seem to "prefer" war; not that we want war itself, but we are blindly and hopelessly attached to all that makes war inevitable.
—Thomas Merton, "Peace: A Religious Responsibility"

"Thank God a child of seven knows what the church is," Martin Luther was fond of saying: "the lambs who hear their Shepherd's voice." Some of the most familiar words in Scripture are these:

I am the good shepherd; the good shepherd lays down his life for the sheep. The hireling, when he sees the wolf coming, abandons the sheep and runs away, because he is no shepherd and the sheep are not his. Then the wolf harries the flock and scatters the sheep. . . . I am the good shepherd; I know my own sheep and my sheep know me—as the Father knows me and I know the Father—and I lay down my life for the sheep. (John 10:11-15)

The Lord is our shepherd, and we are the Lord's sheep. But who is the wolf, who frightens the sheep and terrifies the flock, so that it scatters in all directions? The character of the wolf has special significance today. For the wolf is on the prowl; the wolf's howling keeps us awake at night, and even in the daytime the wolf will not leave us in peace. Indeed, this period in the history of our world may be rightly called "The Day of the Wolf."

There are those who say that we should do away with the category of wolf completely. Some have said that one mark of true greatness is the refusal to recognize anyone as an enemy. You cannot have faith in the Jesus Christ revealed in the New Testament, the argument goes, and allow "enemy" into your vocabulary.[1] Jesus takes our enemies from us, calling even Judas his friend. In Matthew's account of the arrest of Jesus, Judas is addressed in this fashion: "Friend, do what you are here to do" (26:50).

But Jesus said, in his most quoted saying up until the second century, "Love your enemies" (Matthew 5:44), not "Love your friends." It is true that "enemy" is a powerful concept. We need to be very careful how we use it. But "Love your enemies" means you do have enemies. Indeed, you should have enemies. This is how Anastasius Grun, a nineteenth-century Austrian diplomat known for his political poetry, states the issue:

> He has no enemy, you say;
> My friend your boast is poor,
> He who hath mingled in the fray
> Of duty that the brave endure
> Must have made foes. If he has none
> Small is the work that he has done.[2]

"Thou preparest a table before me in the presence of mine enemies" means we are in the presence of enemies. There are a lot of forces out there "like wolves tearing the prey, shedding blood, destroying lives to get dishonest gain" (Ezekiel 22:27 RSV). Sheep must learn to live among wolves.

The Scriptures warn constantly about enemy presence and powers, with reason, tradition, and experience cautioning us similarly. Who was it who said, "Friends come and go; enemies last forever"? They are firing real bullets out there, bullets that can shatter one emotionally, physically, spiritually, and professionally. There is a name ("paranoia") for the condition of fearing something that is not out there. There is even a Bible verse for it:

> They will be gripped with fear,
>   just where there is no need for fear.
>   (Psalm 53:5 NJB)

But there is no name, no Bible verse, no concept for the condition of being without fear of something that *is* out there. Ignorance may be what it says it is, the activity of ignoring. There is a prayer that ends with the words, "Save, O Lord, by love, by pretense, and by fear." The wolf *is* at our door. How do we answer it?

But wait. One should not cry "Wolf!" too quickly. The enemy may not be what we first think it is. Our most dangerous enemy was, is, and ever shall be ourselves. Just as I am my own worst enemy, so the church is its own worst enemy. Jesus redefined "enemy" to feature the enemy within Israel, not just the enemies of the nation. When Jesus became enraged, he did not go beating the politicians and militarists of his day. He targeted the religious establishment. He cleansed the Temple, not the White House. Jesus' call to arms is not first against Moscow or Washington but against Jerusalem; not just against the state but against the church. Before we do all this tub-thumping and street-pounding in public, we ought at least to begin to get our own house in order and to stab awake the conscience of the church to its own guilt and complicity with the powers and principalities of destruction that are at work in its own life. It was exceedingly important to Paul that the church be at peace. "Agree with one another; live in peace" (II Corinthians 13:11); "you must live at peace among yourselves" (I Thessalonians 5:14); "so far as it depends upon you, live peaceably with all" (Romans

12:18 RSV). There are plenty of targets that we should be firing at, instead of each other.

Nor are our enemies simply the ones which have been so defined by the state. How fickle America's definition of "enemy" is can be stated simply in one word: China. Sometimes our nation itself may be an enemy. One of my favorite prayers was given by Samuel Eaton, a Congregationalist minister who disliked the Madisonian foreign policy of the early 1800s. One Sunday morning he prayed before his congregation: "Lord, thou hast commanded us to pray for our enemies; we would therefore pray for the President and Vice-President of these United States." Our enemies are those institutions, people, and forces that keep the will of God from being done on earth. We are rightly afraid of all wild wolves that howl and scatter the sheep—the war wolf, the hunger wolf, the oppression wolf, the exploitation wolf, and the alienation wolf.

But the place for the sheep is among the wolves. Both Matthew 10:16 and Luke 10:3 report Jesus as saying, "Look, I send you out as sheep among wolves." In saying this Jesus stressed two things that sheep-among-wolves must remember. First, their vulnerability: Wolves are dangerous. But our job is to be sheep; Jesus is the Shepherd whose job it is to take care of wolves, and who risks his life for sheep. Second, their victory: We can fear no evil, for "thy rod and thy staff, they comfort [us]" (Psalm 23:4 RSV). Jesus is the Lamb of God whose death and resurrection have made it possible that

> The wolf shall dwell with the lamb
>   and the leopard shall lie down with the kid,
> and the calf and the lion and the fatling together,
>   and a little child shall lead them.
> · (Isaiah 11:6-7 RSV)

"And a little child shall lead them." It is only the leadership of lambs, only the child's virtues of prayer, patience, surprise, parables, peace, love, and the sign of Jonah that will be of any use when confronted by the five wolves scratching at our door and howling for us to come out.

This is the heart of the furor that arose in 1986 over whether to drop "Onward Christian Soldiers" from a new edition of *The United Methodist Hymnal*. Originally, this song was a march written by an Anglican minister for a children's festival in 1864. The composer of the hymn, Sir Arthur Seymour Sullivan, predicted he would be better known for this stirring tune than for all his Gilbert and Sullivan operettas. We have proved him right.

My first reaction to the frenzy was bemusement and bewilderment: bemusement over the spectacle of people, many of whom do little more than move lips during congregational singing, jumping up and down, shouting "Don't you dare take away my hymn"; bewilderment at the massive gall of newspaper columnists and editors, many of whom never set foot inside the door of a church, lambasting the church for its supposed insensitivity and idiocy. Senator George McGovern's campaign manager, Sam Brown, had a wonderful maxim: "Never offend people with style when you can offend them with substance." Which was it? Was the case of the "Threat of the Deleted Hymn" another illustration of Francis Asbury's comment that no people talk so long, so loudly, and so seriously about trifles, as Methodists? Or was something substantive at stake?

What was at stake, and why the commotion may ultimately prove healthy, was that the church was dealing with this issue of how to confront the wolves of the world. Do we do so truly as a church militant, or in some other fashion? Can there be militant metaphors in our songs without a militant theology? Do we meet the forces of evil using their language and terminology, or do we have another language and terminology to use? We have learned, first from Adam then from feminist theologians, the centrality of language: that those who name the world rule the world. So the debate is an important one for us to engage in.

The arguments for the exclusion of militaristic images from Christian conversation are compelling. First of all, the insertion of violent language is a rather poor addition to the world. There is enough violence to begin with, especially without the church adding to the pile. Second, the argument for biblical precedent—the fact that military language is the language of the Bible—will not work, for the same reasons that such a rationale for the use of noninclusive language and imagery does not work. Since the Bible contains everything, it can be misused to justify everything. Third, the structure of military symbols has many drawbacks and limitations and is too easily corruptible. Battle cries very quickly can become battle-axes. It makes adversaries into enemies, puts us immediately into win-lose situations, fosters dualism, gives aid and comfort to *the* Enemy, and what is perhaps the most problematic character of the military-symbol frame, is ultimately triumphalist. Gordon Kaufman has recently launched the most vigorous attack in many years on the traditional symbolism of the Jewish-Christian tradition, for precisely this reason: the unprecedented possibility of nuclear extermination renders many of our traditional formulations not merely irrelevant but harmful.[3] Fourth, military language drags into any discussion all sorts of destructive presuppositions and inappropriate attitudes, which are based more on cultural norms and influences than on Jesus Christ.

With the strength of these arguments, did the compilers of the new United Methodist hymnal make the right decision in recommending that "Onward Christian Soldiers" be retained in the hymnbook? Maybe. If they did so purely as a response to constituency pressures, no. But if they did so based on reasoned and seasoned reflection on the issues at stake, then yes, the right decision was made to keep "Onward Christian

Soldiers." Just as you can have battles without bullets and bombs, so you can have militaristic hymns without a militaristic ethic. The notion that to be antiwar is the same thing as to be antimilitary gives in to the thinking that all the problems of the world yield to military solutions. Paul used militaristic metaphors to deal with a militaristic culture. The early Christians lived under the Pax Romana, which was kept by the show of force. New Testament writers thus used the military metaphor and translated and transformed it into the battle language of the church. "Let Christ Jesus himself be the armor that you wear," Paul writes in Romans 13:14. The most extensive biblical use of military images occurs in the book that has peace as its central theme: the book of Ephesians, where we are told twice in chapter 6 to put on God's armor (6:11, 13).

But we should use military language only with sensitivity and care, knowing that there is danger in using it. One of history's more comic figures was Saint Gerald of Aurillac, a feudal lord who always sent his men into battle backward so that their spears and swords would not hurt anyone deliberately. But even the backward use of weapons was dangerous. Jesus himself found this out. Jesus used analogies and metaphors of war (e.g., Luke 11:21, 14:31). He got into trouble and was misunderstood for using military language. An obscure text that I have never known what to make of until now is Luke 22:35-38.

> He said to them, "When I sent you out barefoot without purse or pack, were you ever short of anything?" "No," they answered. "It is different now," he said; "whoever has a purse had better take it with him, and his pack too; and if he has no sword, let him sell his cloak to buy one. For Scripture says, 'And he was counted among the outlaws,' and these words, I tell you, must find fulfilment in me; indeed, all that is written of me is being fulfilled." "Look, Lord," they said, "we have two swords here." "Enough, enough!" he replied.

Jesus is using the figurative language here of "purse," "Scripture," and "sword" to warn the disciples about a coming spiritual battle that they must prepare to meet. But the disciples take his words literally, and rather stupidly show off their readiness by presenting Jesus with two swords. Jesus turns away in frustration and disgust with the words, "Enough, Enough!" as if to say, "Oh, forget it. You don't have any idea what I'm talking about."

At least at this point in history, singing about "soldiers of Christ" (II Timothy 2:3-4), "armor of God" (Ephesians 6:11), and "[fighting] the good fight" (II Timothy 4:7) are worth the risk. For one thing, we must be careful not to destroy meaningful symbols that give people identity. We must have symbols and metaphors to avoid literalism and idolatry. This is what Jesus did—he took familiar myths and metaphors and invested them with new meaning. The cross, the crux of our story, symbolizes the Christian unwillingness to use the techniques of compulsive power to achieve ends. But the cross itself is a violent military symbol. The sign of the cross, wherever it appears, is a shocking, silent witness to the fact that all instruments of human destruction (the cross, the rack, the iron boot, the crossbow, the gallows, the rifle, germ warfare, the gas oven, the A-bomb, the H-bomb) and all weapons of war can be redeemed and can even become instruments of redemption, through the power of God's love. That is why the cross was and is such a scandal; the first century's equivalent of the bomb was made into a symbol of reconciliation and salvation. Could it be that one of the reasons some of us are nervous about infusing war images with new meaning is that the offense of the gospel is too much for us? We are afraid of being scandalous.

If we were really to live the scandal of Jesus Christ, might we not become crusaders? That word "crusader" literally means "cross-bearer." The problem with the crusades of the Middle Ages was that Christians used the cross as the Romans used it, to kill, and not as Jesus used it, to bear and heal. What the church needs is a new crusade—a crusade of love, a crusade of justice, a crusade of peace. In a sense, what the world needs is not peace, but war; not physical violence against human beings, but spiritual warfare negating all that breeds hostility and division within the human family. "Pacifist though I am," Georgia Harkness once wrote, "I find great vigor in the phrase, 'the church militant.' "[4]

One of the positive attributes of "Onward Christian Soldiers" is its portrayal of a church engaged in spiritual warfare, which, as Saint John Chrysostom put it, "does not make the living dead, but rather makes the dead to rise." Erik Routley wrote in *Hymns and the Faith,* "to sing it ["Onward Christian Soldiers"] presupposes the conviction that the church is, or ought to be, going somewhere, making headway, claiming conquests in the holy war."[5] Harry Emerson Fosdick's great hymn, "God of Grace and God of Glory," prays both "cure thy children's warring madness" and

> Gird our lives, that they may be
> Armored with all Christ-like graces
> In the fight to set men free.

The Christian is summoned to spiritual warfare against the forces of sin and oppression, while physical warfare against people is condemned.[6]

A character in one of Alan Paton's South African novels says of heaven, "When I go up there, which is my intention, the Big Judge will say to me 'Where are your wounds?' And if I say I haven't any He will say 'Was there nothing to fight for?' I couldn't face that question."[7] In the words of Isaac Watts's hymn, "Am I A Soldier of the Cross":

> Are there no foes for me to face?
> Must I not stem the flood?
> Is this vile world a friend to grace[?]
> . . . .
> Sure I must fight, if I would reign;
> Increase my courage, Lord.

The church has declared war on war. There is evil out there that must be fought. As Martin Luther's "A Mighty Fortress Is Our God" reminds us,

> our ancient foe
> Doth seek to work us woe;
> His craft and power are great.

There are forces at work that are at war with God. Jesus believed in the existence of evil. Every New Testament writer is a dualist, and we should suffer no embarrassment in subscribing to a dualism where evil is luciferic but not satanic. In satanic dualism, evil is an original, opposing force to God. There is a good god and an evil god. In luciferic dualism, evil is a form of fallen good.

The Bible believes in peace through strength: "The God of peace will soon crush Satan beneath your feet" (Romans 16:20). Colossians 2:13-15 says:

> For he has forgiven us all our sins; he has cancelled the bond which pledged us to the decrees of the law. It stood against us, but he has set it aside, nailing it to the cross. On that cross he discarded the cosmic powers and authorities like a garment; he made a public spectacle of them and led them as captives in his triumphal procession.

But a biblical peace-through-strength approach does not lead to a build-up of nuclear research or strategic power. If God is love, then God will confront evil and oppose it in loving ways, certainly not through the shooting war glorified in "The Battle Hymn of the Republic" or through the violent duel portrayed in Carman's contemporary gospel hit, "The Champion." The events of Holy Week describe a Holy War. The sequence all four Gospels agree on—triumphal entry, cleansing of the Temple, Last Supper, crucifixion, resurrection—is a battle sequence against evil. The strength of weakness, the power of powerlessness, the security of insecurity are revealed in an old poem entitled "The Conquerors," by Harry Kemp, which compares history's most mighty military rules, such as Genghis Khan, Alexander the Great, Caesar, and Napoleon, with one of history's most powerless figures, Jesus Christ. The poem ends with these words:

> Then all they perished from the earth
>   As fleeting shadows from a glass,
> And conquering down the centuries,
>   Came Christ, the Swordless, on an ass![8]

The church is less served with an image of "wimps of Christ, lie down," than "soldiers of Christ, arise." Even hell was not designed for mice. It can be right to fight. To be a pacifist is not to be a pacifier. Pacifism does not mean an unwillingness to fight but a willingness to engage in new forms of fighting. Peacemakers need to have fight in them, which is another reason why "Onward Christian Soldiers" has its place. It is a corrective to the image of "gentle Jesus, meek and mild." Think about it. Jesus disturbed the peace before he distributed the peace. As William Langland wrote in *Piers Plowman,* this gentle Jesus will "joust." The notion that because Christ is the Prince of Peace, all language speaking of conflict should be forbidden and erased is contradicted by hundreds of passages in the Bible, not the least of which quotes Jesus himself: "I have not come to bring peace, but a sword" (Matthew 10:34).

But Jesus' sword is not something the Pentagon would know anything about, nor something the Pentagon would know how to use. Combat spirituality is not what everyone thinks it is. "And if Yahweh strikes Egypt, having struck he will heal," Isaiah 19:22 (NJB) reads. Here is one amazing sword; a sword that doesn't draw blood, indeed, a sword that heals as it hits. In the great tradition of Quaker pacifism, early Quaker theologians developed the doctrine of "the Lamb's

War," drawing on a metaphor found in the book of Revelation. They said that Christ took the Old Testament concept of the Warrior Yahweh and its holy-war talk and turned it on its head. Vernard Eller, in his marvelous little book reprinted a few years back, *War and Peace from Genesis to Revelation,* calls Christ's way of fighting, this Lamb's way of fighting that overcomes the world, "reverse fighting."[9] The classic battle in the Lamb's War has already taken place at Skull Hill. There Jesus won by losing; there Jesus lived by dying; there Jesus fought by not fighting; there victory went to the one who shed his own blood rather than shed the blood of his enemies.

In the Lamb's War, suffering servanthood is the means of fighting. Indeed, there is but one way of fighting—not laying down someone else's life, but laying down one's own life. In the Lamb's War, the war-horse is a donkey, a beast of burden, not a stallion, a beast of brutality. In the Lamb's War, there is the church militant, but its militancy is in loving God with all our might, soul, and strength, and our neighbor as ourselves. In the Lamb's War, "confrontation" does not mean a bloody battle. Breaking the word down, confrontation means simply "to put in front." Confrontation is putting Christ's ways in front of evil's way. In the Lamb's War, people are not the enemy. "Hate what is evil," Romans 12:9 (RSV) reads, not hate the evildoer. The Lamb's War is fought *for* people, not *against* people. It is not who we are fighting, but what we are fighting—demonic forces, without and within: prejudice, fear, hatred, selfishness—that is the enemy of humanity.

In the Lamb's War, there are only weapons of peace. Paul wrote, "For though we live in the world we are not carrying on a worldly war, for the weapons of our warfare are not worldly but have divine power to destroy strongholds. We destroy arguments and every proud obstacle to the knowledge of God, and take every thought captive to obey Christ" (II Corinthians 10:3-5 RSV).

The Lamb's War calls for unworldly weapons like *prayer*. The best way to learn to love enemies is to pray for them. In *Against Celsus,* Origen had this to say:

> For we [Christians] no longer take up "sword against nation," nor do we "learn [to make] war any more," having become children of peace for the sake of Jesus who is our leader. . . . and no one fights better for the king than we do. We do not indeed fight under him although he require it, but we fight on his behalf, forming a special army, an army of piety, by offering our prayers to God.[10]

Christians cannot be soldiers of the king, Origen is saying. But they can be even more valuable and powerful than soldiers, by fighting with their prayers. Acts 4:31 (RSV) graphically portrays the released reality of prayer: "And when they had prayed, the place in which they were gathered together was shaken." Prayer can shake up places like Washington and Moscow, directing them to paths they had no intention of following. We must not wait until a mushroom cloud appears on the horizon to pray for peace with all our heart.

The Lamb's War calls for unworldly weapons like *surprise*. In the Lamb's War, the element of surprise is essential. The tactic of surprise, which is at the heart of the Sermon on the Mount, catches our enemies off guard. They expect us to retaliate, and in fact have built a total national security foundation on the principle of retaliation, not just of the eye-for-an-eye, tooth-for-a-tooth variety but of the nation-for-an-eye, creation-for-a-tooth variety. But we surprise them. We outwit the opposition by refusing to retaliate, by giving them more than they wanted and bargained for. You want my shirt? Here it is, and take my coat as well. You want me to carry something for you a mile? I'll carry it two (Matthew 5:38-42). Or look at Luke 10:4, a wonderful example of the weapon of surprise at work. Jesus says that sometimes we should "exchange no greetings on the road."

Sometimes peacemakers should shock people by not giving them the customary greeting of peace, to draw attention to the absence of peace. As Erik Erikson puts it in a little known but extremely significant article, "The Galilean Sayings and the Sense of 'I' ":

> Nonviolent behavior must often be shocking in order to shake up the violent opponent's seemingly so normal attitude, to make him feel that his apparently undebatable and spotless advantage in aggressive initiative is being taken away from him and that he is being forced to overdo his own action absurdly.[11]

The Lamb's War requires unworldly weapons like *restraint*. The German biblical scholar Ernst Fuchs lamented some years ago that the only thing New Testament scholars had discovered in the last fifty years was the fact that Jesus had spoken in parables. It was one of the most important things they could have learned. Jesus used the parable in confrontations because it was a weapon of restraint: It preserved his enemies' freedom to choose, thus respecting their personhood and right of self-determination. It also demonstrated that sometimes we best promote peace by *not* saying our piece. Just as Jesus restrained the pace of events in John 8:1-11 by writing on the sand, so Jesus spoke in parables to teach his most important lessons, thus restraining our thought patterns from their routine-ridden ruts. Ultimately, people are not persuaded by powerful logic or even organized effort. This is "the intellectual fallacy," the mistaken belief that sound argumentation buttressed by indisputable facts and efficient planning is sufficient to decide any matter at hand. Rather, people are persuaded by halting the mind's inertia, and by showing enthusiasm for new ways of thinking and of perceiving reality.

The Lamb's War entails unworldly weapons like *peace itself*. There is an old saying: "There is no way to peace, because peace is the way." The only true path to peace is peace. Peace is a condition brought about by being peaceful. Peace is an achievement of people who live the gospel truth, "Resist not evil, return good for evil." We can always find ways to justify returning evil for evil, as Jesus reminded us in his handling of the question about divorce (Matthew 19:3-9). Imagine:

People: What about war, Mr. Jesus? What about Hitler and his kind?

Jesus: What does Moses say?

People: Moses says if they threaten God's plans, then it is a holy war, a just war—so knock their blocks off!

Jesus: Moses wrote that because of *your* hardness of heart; but *in the beginning, God . . .*

In short, there is another way.

Peace is a by-product of the refusal to do evil or be violent, and the living out of a lifestyle of love, justice, and peace. The idea that governments rest on force is one of those half-truths that beget total lies. For governments ultimately do not rest on force. Even repressive governments rest on, or require in some degree, the consent of the governed. The greatest weapon any people have, and the one weapon that can never be taken away from them, is the weapon of consent. The cement that holds a society together is its consensus, its belief system, its myth structure. Power is effective only in acquiescence. When people withdraw consent or subscribe to a different belief system, power is dethroned. Not even the magnetism and charisma of Hitler would have succeeded without the willingness of followers. If Christians had resisted the militarist Nazi mind-set from the start and challenged the civil religion of the Third Reich, Hitler would never have gotten as far as he did to begin with. And Christian withdrawal of consent from the Hitler regime would have, over the long haul, brought down the state. Power is not only in the hands of politicians and bureaucrats. Public opinion and popular culture are the real decision-makers. The only true path to peace is the way of peace, the way of people not giving in to violence and hatred.

Theorist Gene Sharp, director of the Center for Nonviolent Sanctions at Harvard University, strategist Howard S. Brembeck, president of the Alternative World Foundation, and activist Liane Norman, cofounder of the River City Nonviolent Resistance Campaign, have understood far better than the church the lessons of the church's own history: that the catacombs ultimately triumph over the coliseum. Sharp, Brembeck, and Norman are preoccupied with politics, defense, and the nonviolent use of power. Brembeck's "Civilized Defense Plan" advocates the abolition of all offensive weapons by international law and the enforcement of economic sanctions to insure that the law is upheld. Sharp and Norman have demonstrated that what Sharp calls "Civilian Based Defense" and what Norman calls "Citizen Intervention" (she prefers this to "civil disobedience") have much more power to prevent war, sabotage oppressive governments, and undermine morale than violent forms of defense and resistance.[12] Norman's favorite example is that of a two-year-old child who resists having a snowsuit put on. The most powerful adult can be overcome by frustration, brought to his or her knees and reduced to the brink of tears by a simple act of noncompliance.

There is a vast array of psychological, economical, social, and political nonviolent-resistance campaigns—all the way from symbolic protests, strikes, economic boycotts, and social disruption to furtively switching street signs and inviting Russian soldiers in for dinner. But what is common to all scenarios in which a society commits itself to "transarmament" (a gradual phasing in of civilian-based deterrence and defense as a supplement to and eventually substitute for military-based deterrence and defense) is that the power of persuasion (Gandhi) or coercion (Sharp) over the power of violence brings both a double refusal and a double victory. The double refusal is the refusal to hate the enemy and the refusal to obey the enemy. The double victory is the eventual overcoming of the enemy and the winning of that enemy as a friend. There will be casualties in nonviolent resistance. But the weapon of peace is far less costly of human life than the weapon of war.

The double refusal and double victory at work can be seen in Carl Sandburg's four-volume study of Abraham Lincoln, which reveals a remarkable relationship that grew up between President Lincoln and the steady stream of Quakers who visited him at the White House.[13] The president frustrated his friends and advisors in seeing so many people with complaints and needs—he called them his "public opinion baths"—but Lincoln appeared even more open and available to Quakers than to nearly anyone else. Quaker teaching stood at loggerheads with Lincoln on two points. First, the Quakers hated war and thought the President should end the hostilities. Second, they hated slavery. Since the President had not yet issued an emancipation order, they presented memorials and other such petitions in hopes of changing his mind toward immediately issuing one.

One joins Lincoln's advisors in wondering why the President chose to see these delegations at all. The Quakers were politically unimportant. He certainly did not need to be worn down by political lobbyists any more than he was. But see them he did. We don't know what went on at these meetings, but we do know that the same group of Quakers came back regularly in following weeks. And there were almost regular visits to the White House from Quakers. What happened at these meetings? Perhaps Lincoln and the Quakers prayed together, or simply sat in silence together— "in meeting" as the Quakers call it, listening for God's lead. But whatever went on, it appears that these parties who should have been in opposing corners found a sustaining strength stronger than either of their privately held positions. These times with the Quakers became a source of continual spiritual renewal for the president, through the grinding and brutalizing years of the Civil War. And within a month after these "Progressive Friends" proposed a course of action that would lead to immediate emancipation, President Lincoln set in motion the very strategy they had recommended to him.

The Lamb's War deploys unworldly weapons like *enemy-love*. Over and over again, we find this Messiah who "guide[s] our feet into the way of peace" (Luke 1:79), taking the initiative and going on the offensive. Sometimes the offensive was physical, as when he cleansed the Temple. Other times the offensive was verbal, as when Jesus, after being struck by a soldier on the cheek (John 18:19-24), protested police brutality (in apparent contradiction of his own teaching about turning the other cheek). On another occasion, Jesus delivered a blistering attack on the Pharisees (Matthew 23:13-33). Sometimes peacemakers are not so much pacifiers as troublemakers, prone to deliberate acts of provocation.

The Sermon on the Mount is less a handbook on how to retreat from the violence of our world than a charter and chart of practical, surprising initiatives for the building of shalom communities: When enemies curse you, go get them and bless them; when enemies persecute you, invite them in for supper; when an enemy forces you to carry a pack a long distance, carry it twice as long and see if you can't effect some reconciliation on the way; when someone is saying nasty things about you, talk to him or her personally and see what you can learn about yourself; when someone hits you on one side of your face, don't just refrain from not getting even, but take the surprising initiative of turning the other cheek. It is a consistent biblical witness: Peacemakers are those who take the initiative.

Of course, love your enemies, a simple formula of only three words in English, four words in Greek, is the greatest initiative of them all. There is an old Chinese proverb: "If thine enemy offend thee, buy each of his children a drum." Jesus found the seeds of enemy-love in Judaism and let them grow into the very trunk of his ethical teaching. The cross demonstrates how God deals with enemies: through suffering love.

There is no shallow notion of peace in enemy-love. You don't give up power when you love enemies—you use it differently, redemptively and cooperatively. Peacemakers are people who fight with power. First Corinthians 4:20 (NIV) reads: "The kingdom of God is not a matter of talk but of power." And the most powerful weapon we have is love. Jesus said, "Love your enemies." Why? Because it's the absolute worst thing you could do to them. Romans 12:14-21 has been called the great pacifist paragraph of the New Testament. It concludes with Paul quoting from the book of Proverbs: "But there is another text: 'If your enemy is hungry, feed him; if he is thirsty, give him a drink; by doing this you will heap live coals on his head.' Do not let evil conquer you, but use good to defeat evil."

Even though enemy-love is God's answer to evil, love will not always be returned. Love does not always beget love. Love is not necessarily a reciprocal relationship. I shall never forget reading in college a collection of essays edited by Abraham Maslow in which Pitirim A. Sorokin writes on his research into the power produced by creative, unselfish love. "Without a notable increase of what we call creative unselfish love in man and in the human universe, all fashionable prescriptions for prevention of wars and for building of a new order cannot achieve their purpose." Love was effective in resolving conflict in about 75–85 percent of the cases he studied.[14] But even this sanguine study admits that love will not be returned almost 25 percent of the time. In other words, we give love knowing full well that love may never be returned.

There is nothing utilitarian about enemy-love. Enemy-loving is indiscriminate (Matthew 5:45) and unconditional. We love our enemies not because it works but because it is the truth. You *may* make enemies into friends by loving them, which is the ultimate in "winning," but you may also make them even more your enemies. In this new crusade for peace, cross-bearers fight with enemy-love, knowing they have nothing to lose but their lives. The crusade of cross-bearing is a heroic notion. Peace requires greater heroism than war.

The only thing a cross is good for is to die on. A cross is not a burden; a cross is a death. And a crusader as a cross-bearer is one who is prepared to give martyr witness to peace. There can be a high cost to cross-bearing for peace. In no place in the Gospels does Jesus beg people to join him. Many times Jesus warns people about the high cost of discipleship, warns them about what it means to be a follower of Jesus Christ, warns them to stay away if they can't drink the bitter cup.

We love, knowing full well we get nothing in return except maybe death, because God's nature is love (Luke 6:35). We love not because enemies deserve our love but because enemies *need* our love. There is a wonderful fable that tells of a young girl walking through a meadow who sees a butterfly impaled upon a thorn. Very carefully she releases it, and the butterfly flies away. Then it comes back and changes into a beautiful angel. "For your kindness," the angel tells the little girl, "I will grant you your fondest wish." The little girl thought for a moment, and then replied: "I want to be happy." The angel leaned toward her and whispered in her ear and then suddenly vanished.

As the girl grew, no one in the land was happier than she. Whenever anyone asked her for the secret of her happiness, she would only smile and say, "I listened to an angel." As she grew quite old, the neighbors were afraid the fabulous secret might die with her. "Tell us, please," they begged. "Tell us what the angel said." The now lovely old lady simply smiled and said, "She told me that everyone, no matter how secure they seemed, has need of me." We love because everyone has need of our love. In fact, even God has need of our love. Even God has chosen to need us. Only a poet, Rainer Maria Rilke, dared capture this vision in a poem.

> What will you do, God, when I die?
> When I, your pitcher, broken, lie?
> When I, your drink, go stale or dry?
> I am your garb, the trade you ply,
> you lose your meaning, losing me.
>
> Homeless without me, you will be
> robbed of your welcome, warm and sweet.
> I am your sandals: your tired feet
> will wander bare for want of me.
>
> Your mighty cloak will fall away.
> Your glance that on my cheek was laid
> and pillowed warm, will seek, dismayed,
> the comfort that I offered once—
> to lie, as sunset colors fade
> in the cold lap of alien stones.
>
> What will you do, God? I am afraid.[15]

Finally, the Lamb's War gathers to the cause unworldly weapons like the *sign of Jonah*. When the Pharisees challenged Jesus to show them a sign, Jesus built on the Jonah story in this way: "It is a wicked, godless generation that asks for a sign; and the only sign that will be given it is the sign of the prophet Jonah" (see Matthew 12:38-41 and Luke 11:29-32). What is the mysterious "sign of Jonah" given to a "wicked, godless generation"? This is a difficult pericope, and no one has yet succeeded in giving a satisfactory rendition of it. In fact, Matthew itself suggests two different explanations. In Matthew 12:40, the story of Jonah is a prolepsis of the death, descent into hell, and resurrection of Jesus Christ. In Matthew 12:41, the sign of Jonah is Jesus himself. An examination of both interpretations reveals a great deal about what it means to fight on the front lines of the Lamb's War.

In Matthew 12:40, the sign of Jonah is the resurrection of our Lord and our ability to live as risen Christians. This means that God gives the church, like Jonah thrown overboard by Phoenician sailors, the gifts of indigestibility, unsinkability, and illimitability. Indigestibility is the church's resistance to being consumed by the world, even after taking up residence in its very belly. Jesus' refusal to give a sign represents his rebuking the use of standard scribal categories to understand his ministry. Jesus' contemporaries wanted to judge him according to norms laid out by scribal interpretation. Jesus rejected this way of signs, both because it accented container over content and because it violated a personal response and decision about revelation. Called to be "in the world" but not "of the world," Jesus expects the church to follow its own way of life rather than conform to worldly patterns. "Friendship with the world is enmity with God," James 4:4 (RSV) declares.

In this Constantinian era in which American churches find themselves, indigestibility is not a popular trait. We stress involvement in the world to the point of integration into it. We are afraid of "separatist" or "escapist" mentalities and do not like to be set aside from the currents of the age. But the Constantinian effect on the church has always been negative, and by the time the world's digestive juices have done their work, the church is left with nothing distinctive or nourishing to contribute. The prospect of culture vomiting us out is not one of the more appealing for our future. But only a diaspora model of life, with Christians as pilgrims instead of residents, can present to the world what it most needs: a living testimony to another way than the world's way, an alternative model to living by terror and threat. The world of the church, for all cultures, should be fundamentally alien and socially disruptive.

The church is more than a witness to the resurrection; it is also an agent of resurrection, returning life to life. We owe it to the world to be ourselves and to not budge from the position Wesley penned to Francis Asbury in 1788: "Let the Presbyterians do what they please, but let the Methodists know their calling better."[16] The first- and second-century church envisioned itself as a "contrast community," in the words of Gerhard Lohfink.[17] When challenged by evil empires and sea monster bellies, the church finds its best defense in its indigestibility.

If indigestibility shows us how to survive intact in the belly of the whale, unsinkability demonstrates that regurgitation leads to resurrection. The Emperor Nero is supposed to have sent his own mother to sea in a Roman galley. His motives were far from the best, as he arranged to have holes bored in the ship's hull. In spite of these and other machinations, the indomitable woman stayed afloat and survived. It was said of her by early chroniclers that she showed "unsinkability." The sign of Jonah is our "unsinkability."

We can risk defeat, even death in the whale's belly, because we know that God can pull off resurrections. The greatest power in the universe (and the strongest arms for the disarmed) is the power of resurrection. The church must not be into winning but into fighting for Christ. Yet losing does not turn us into connoisseurs of despair, for the sign of Jonah is never missing. We have enough people who read despair into Scripture; the church needs people who read Scripture into despair. And when one begins reading Scripture into one's despair, one stops whining things like "the chimes of midnight are already sounding," "this is the Eleventh Hour," or "the chief problem of our time is the problem of time." The hands of the clock are not ticking. The Eleventh Hour is passed. The chimes of midnight have already sounded. The victory, we are promised, is ours. No confinement, no entombment, no vanquishment can keep us down. The ultimate inversion in this crazy reverse fighting of Jesus' is that his followers are fighting a war backward.

The victory is already won. "The Lamb will conquer them," Revelation 17:14 (RSV) announces. Jesus' work was completed through his death and resurrection, when Jesus conquered death once and for all and emerged from the tomb triumphant. The followers of Jesus find themselves in the enviable position of being in the midst of the consequences of Jesus' victory being worked out, of being sent into play when the game is already in the bag. Our battle song is not "We shall overcome someday" but "God has overcome this day."

There is a passage in Judges that reads: "Then Deborah said to Barak, 'Up! This day the Lord gives Sisera into your hands. Already the Lord has gone out to battle before you' " (4:14-15). In other words, Deborah is saying: Hurry up, or God will finish the job before you even set foot on the field of battle. Then you will miss the joy and blessing of being a part of the victory. Or as this is stated most classically in the Old Testament, "Yahweh has given the enemy into your hands."

The dragon has already been slain. In the words of Vernard Eller, "Far from becoming anxious and frustrated over the seeming intransigence of the industrial-military complex and the apparent impossibility of making any perceptible dent upon the world, the Christian peacemaker knows that the monster already has been decapitated by the sharp two-edged sword of Jesus."[18] The temptation of Saint George is to slay dragons that have already been defeated.

We track dragons to their lairs of loneliness, hatred, rapacity, and selfishness, only to forget that the monster inside is sick unto death. Our calling is to shout at people who have fallen into graves of gloom: "Get up"; "take up your bed and walk"; "walk on that water"; "Christ is risen"; "you are a new, living being"; "rejoice and be exceeding glad." Our mission is to join with the character in Eugene O'Neil's play *Lazarus Laughed,* whose constant refrain was: "Laugh with me! Death is dead! Fear is no more! There is only life! There is only laughter!"[19] A new book on the Alps begins by calling them "the magic mountains where nothing ever seems impossible."[20] Our job is to announce that Christians live in an alpine world where resurrection makes mountains "magic" and where "nothing ever seems impossible." The most amazing and incredible story (which is Webster's definition of the big "fish story") since Jonah and the whale is the story of the ways in which, with Christ, all things are possible (Philippians 4:13).

I will never forget when Cesar Chavez gathered his supporters after they had lost their campaign in California to pass Proposition 14. Together they took a long day's journey into night, partying and celebrating until the wee hours of the morning. A reporter who witnessed the spectacle said, "My God, think what it would have been like if they had won." Standards of success and failure no longer have the same meaning for the peacemaker. Peacemakers do not have to worry about winning and losing, success and failure.

Peacemakers only have to worry about accepting God's victory on God's terms. Joshua's statement of this cannot be paraphrased better: "Take very good care to love Yahweh your God." These words come from the last words in the last speech Joshua ever gave the children of Israel:

> You must hold fast to the Lord your God as you have done down to this day. For your sake the Lord has driven out great and mighty nations; to this day not a man of them has

withstood you. One of you can put to flight a thousand, because the Lord your God fights for you, as he promised. Be on your guard then, love the Lord your God. (Joshua 23:8-11)

The third feature of the sign of Jonah is the illimitability of Christian love. Ninevah was synonymous with God's worst enemy, a foreign nation that symbolized every cruelty, injustice, barbarism, and licentiousness known to the Near Eastern world. But in the figures of Jonah and the Ninevites one sees reflected God's inexhaustible patience with a person and a people, and a love that never lets go. God should destroy enemies, we think, not forgive them. But God loves enemies while fighting them. God loves the devil, even while taming the devil's evil ways.[21] No limitations can be set on the love of God. There can be no pulling back on God's reach, even toward the worst offenders. Not willing that any should perish, God is calling us to fight for the liberation not just of our allies but of our archenemies as well. The resurrectionary, unconquerable power of God and the unbounded mercy of God jeopardize the "just deserts" of all modern Ninevahs (Leningrad, Los Angeles, Moscow, and Washington) and all modern Ninevites (Kadhafi, Khomeni, Duvalier).

Assuredly, the very thought of Hitler in heaven is revolting. But no more revolting than the thought of the "kings of the earth" inhabiting the New Jerusalem, to the early, persecuted Christians. In chapter 16 of the book of Revelation, the unholy trinity of dragon, beast, and false prophet join forces with the devil's first volunteers, the "kings of the earth," and assemble their respective armies at Armageddon. Here they await the beginning of the final battle with God's forces, only to have them never show up. The Battle of Armageddon is won simply by the voice of God announcing from the clouds, "It is over!" (Revelation 16:17). What is so disturbing to our sensibilities and sense of justice, however, is that these very same "kings of the earth," the

Neros and Domitians of the world, show up in the place where every tear is wiped away and death is no more.

> I saw no temple in the city; for its temple was the sovereign Lord God and the Lamb. And the city had no need of sun or moon to shine upon it, for the glory of God gave it light, and its lamp was the Lamb. By its light shall the nations walk, and the kings of the earth shall bring into it all their splendour. The gates of the city shall never be shut by day—and there will be no night. (Revelation 21:22-25)

As Vernard Eller comments on this passage:

> With us the victory of the good guys always means the defeat and destruction of the bad guys. But when the winner is King Jesus, he brings the losers—even those God damned (so we had assumed) kings of the earth, and them in all their splendor—right into the victory circle with him.[22]

Jesus used the sign of Jonah to distinguish himself from false prophets and to reveal how his holy war is waged against the powers of Beelzebub. The sign of Jonah may have another meaning. John Howton has demonstrated that in Aramaic the word Jonah also means "the dove." Thus our simple transliteration in Greek may obscure Jesus' deeper promise of the "sign of the dove," a Jewish symbol for Israel as the messenger of God's redemptive purpose.[23] In offering the sign of the dove, Jesus is presenting himself as a summary source for the fulfillment of God's purposes in the world, a fulfillment Jews had come to expect solely from the nation of Israel. The sign of the dove, then, is Jesus himself. "For he is himself our peace," states one of the most moving passages in the Bible. All our peace programs and war pogroms must be subject to this confession:

> For he himself is our peace. Gentiles and Jews, he has made the two one, and in his own body of flesh and blood has broken down the enmity which stood like a dividing wall between

them; for he annulled the law with its rules and regulations, so as to create out of the two a single new humanity in himself, thereby making peace. (Ephesians 2:14-15)

Peace is Christ himself, the gift to those united with Christ and to Christ. Peace is not an axiom or ordinance or principle. Peace is a person. Peace is not the principle of "God is love." Peace is the person of Jesus Christ, who announces to the world the never-ending story of "God loves you."

No matter how sad it may be to see a once-fearsome wolf with its teeth pulled, the Lamb's War has been won. The sign of the dove ends the day and way of the wolf.

CHAPTER 4

Stalking Wild Turkeys
in Tiger Country

Borrowed Gods erased the soul and left you with nothing you could call your own.
—D. H. Lawrence, *The Plumed Serpent*

Ever bought a fake picture? . . . The more you pay for it, the less inclined you are to doubt it.
—John Le Carré, *Tinker, Tailor, Soldier, Spy*

If you are stalking wild turkeys in tiger country, you must always keep your eyes peeled for tigers. But when you stalk for tigers, you can ignore the turkeys. We live in tiger country, but so far in this book we have been content to stalk turkeys. It is time to search out bigger game. Wild turkeys can take care of themselves.

The arms race is at bottom an issue of graven images: Who is the true God? The Bible talks about those who "feared the Lord but also served their own Gods" (II Kings 17:33 RSV), those who "bow down and swear to the Lord and yet swear by Milcom" (Zephaniah 1:5 RSV). The human mind is, according to John Calvin, "a veritable factory of idols," churning out idol after idol of "manufactured gods," produced "to get permission to do the things which our real God forbids us to do."[1] The fundamental sin propelling the arms race forward, therefore, is not atheism but polytheism, not antichrists but what are even more dangerous, mini-Christs. The social employment of Christians as god-builders has led to the rebuilding of Babel rather than to the reversal of its consequences. This chapter is about idolatry, or in the words of the Scottish ragtime poem, "The Gods That I Know Best."[2] This chapter is also about what Christians can expect when they confront tigers, and the violence that can be roused when the vested interests of those idols are disturbed.

One of the most exciting episodes in the Acts account of Paul's missionary journeys was the riot at Ephesus, narrated in chapter 19. The preaching of this tentmaker from Tarsus was threatening virtually every idol of the ancient world, the most powerful of which were economics and politics. Once before, the gospel's threat to idolatry nearly cost Paul his life. Paul and Silas were thrown into jail at Philippi because the owners of an income-producing slave-girl suffered severe financial setbacks after Paul cast out her sooth-saying demon (Acts 16:16-24). But it is the story of the Ephesian riot that best prepares us to see the full panoply of false gods, the way these gods stick together and protect each other, the false security of every false god, the essentially pagan character of our own cultural context, and the effect false gods have upon their worshipers.

> There was a man named Demetrius, a silversmith who made silver shrines of [Artemis] and provided a great deal of employment for the craftsmen. He called a meeting of these men and the workers in allied trades, and addressed them. "Men," he said, "you know that our high standard of living depends on this industry. And you see and hear how this fellow Paul with his propaganda has perverted crowds of people, not only at Ephesus but also in practically the whole of the province of Asia. He is telling them that gods made by human hands are not gods at all. There is danger for us here; it is not only that our line of business will be discredited, but also that the sanctuary of the great goddess [Artemis] will cease to command respect; and then it will not be long before she who is worshipped by all Asia and the civilized world is brought down from her divine pre-eminence."
> When they heard this they were roused to fury and shouted, "Great is [Artemis] of the Ephesians!" The whole city was in

confusion; they seized Paul's travelling-companions, the Macedonians Gaius and Aristarchus, and made a concerted rush with them into the theatre. Paul wanted to appear before the assembly but the other Christians would not let him. Even some of the dignitaries of the province, who were friendly towards him, sent and urged him not to venture into the theatre. Meanwhile some were shouting one thing, some another; for the assembly was in confusion and most of them did not know what they had all come for. But some of the crowd explained the trouble to Alexander, whom the Jews had pushed to the front, and he, motioning for silence, attempted to make a defence before the assembly. But when they recognized that he was a Jew, a single cry arose from them all: for about two hours they kept on shouting, "Great is [Artemis] of the Ephesians!" (Acts 19:24-34)

The drama comes to a climax when the mayor calms the crowd and averts a riot by assuring them that Artemis is too great to be seriously challenged by such a puny threat as Paul presents and that their business will be even more seriously undermined if the government gets wind of a riot in Ephesus. In the "godding up" of religion through Artemis, of the nation through Ephesus, of economics through Demetrius, of politics through the mayor, of security through the Asiarchs, of crowd-pleasing through the mob, we come face to face with "the gods we know best."

The Idol of Religion

The Greeks knew her as Artemis, the Latins, as Diana. The cult of *Artemis Ephesia* was the integrating force of the culture in which much of early Christianity found itself. Artemis herself was an Anatolian mother-goddess and patroness of the city of Ephesus, where her Ionian temple, the great cathedral of paganism, built of marble blocks said to have been held together by gold instead of mortar, stood as one of the seven wonders of the ancient world. As an Asiatic divinity of fertility, her festivals were celebrated accordingly, with wild orgies and violent games. But Artemis herself was no beautiful lady; excavations at Ephesus have unearthed statues of grotesque proportion, the upper portion of her body a profusion of egg-shaped breasts (or rows of ostrich eggs), symbols of fertility, her head flanked by sculptured sphinxes, lions tatooed on her upper arms, and the lower portion of her body made of pillars wrapped in a tight skirt that is ornamented with a phalanx of power symbols: stags, sphinxes, and lions. Artemis' popularity was so immense that Demetrius somewhat extravagantly called her the one "whom all Asia and the world worship." With everyone else paying her homage, the presence of even a few who did not, such as Paul and his companions Gaius and Aristarchus, was especially noticeable and grating. So much so that for two hours the Ephesians chanted in the theater, a place that could hold twenty-nine thousand people, the prayer "Great is Artemis," defying the Christians' effrontery to their god.

Religion can become idolatrous. In Jeremiah 7:1-11, the Israelites cried out like the Ephesians, "the Temple of the Lord, the Temple of the Lord, the Temple of the Lord." In so doing they forgot how ritual is connected to right conduct. When religion becomes an end and not a means to glorifying and serving God, it becomes a false god capable of some of the most heinous destruction imaginable. The religion of Jim Jones and the People's Temple offers graphic illustration of Michael Polanyi's concept of "moral inversion," whereby morally impassioned action can ride roughshod over morality itself. Paul's exposure to idolatry was the false gods of religion—the temptations within our own souls and the sins that dwell within our own households of faith.

The Idol of Nation

Ephesus was not only the "keeper of the sacred stone that fell from the sky" (Acts 19:37 RSV, probably a meteorite roughly in the form of a woman). Ephesus was also the *neokonos* of the emperor, a title officially bestowed by the Roman government on cities loyal to the imperial cult, which were centers for emperor worship. In Ephesian devotion, the worship of Artemis and the emperor were intertwined, making Paul's preaching doubly dangerous, for it struck directly at the heart of the most cherished values of the empire.[5] Little wonder that one of the cries uttered at Ephesus had also attended Paul's ministry in Thessalonica: "These men who have turned the world upside down have come here also" (Acts 17:6-7 RSV).

The idolatry of nation has proven to be one of the strongest forces in the world. Between 1970 and 1985, the stockpile of atomic weaponry in the U.S. has grown by 275 percent; in the Soviet Union, by 533 percent. Both nations' arsenals now hold over ten thousand weapons, the smallest of which is said to be larger than that used on Hiroshima. The Soviet Union's nuclear expenditures are breaking the back of its economy. But the money continues to be directed to the military because of the supremacy of the Bomb as the symbol of the nation's status as a world superpower. Soviet fear of foreigners constitutes an entirely rational response to a thousand years of Russian history. Now, for the first time in that history, they possess military parity with every friend and enemy; any price is worth paying to keep that edge. A religion of "Caesar first" is equally pervasive in America today, where an idolatrous concoction of capitalism and democracy has given rise to the messianic "America first" and "America saves" mentality. In the widely quoted words of Senator Richard Russell, "If we have to start over with another Adam and Eve, I want them to be Americans."

Two stories will suffice to illustrate the way in which nationalism can become a religion. During a particularly pious phase of my college years, I worked in the shipping department of a textile mill (read "sweatshop"), where my co-workers were in the habit of swearing and taking the Lord's name in vain at every turn. Robert Bellah's classic article, "American Civil Religion," had just been published. As a budding historian, I decided to test his thesis about the existence, alongside of our faith religion, of a piety centering on the myths and symbols of the nation. So when I was frustrated with something, instead of uttering "Goddamn it," like many of my co-workers, I began to mutter "America-damn it." Very quickly I earned the reputation for being a vulgar, vile person. I was scorned by my co-workers for my blasphemous and unpatriotic behavior.

A second indication of the idolatry of nation can be found at the United States Air Force Chapel in Colorado Springs. Inside is a cross hung as a mobile. Looked at from one angle, the cross is a sword. Looked at from another angle, the cross-sword is an airplane. Looked at from still another angle, the cross-sword-plane is a dove. The use of a religious symbol to convey double meanings—salvation (cross) and destruction (sword), peace (dove) and war (plane)—is not limited to the Christian faith. But it is especially rampant in a nation that sees itself as a savior of the world, a nation where patriotism has been adulterated as the moral dudgeon of Stephen Decatur's 1816 declaration, "May she always be in the right; but our country, right or wrong."

In spite of the alleged centrality of just-war theory to American Christians, the absence of just-war thinking throughout the course of American history is striking. The thinking of the church in times of war is virtually indistinguishable from that of other social systems. In the book *Wars of America,* we are shown how Christians became eager instruments of propaganda campaigns which helped instigate war and instill hatred among the masses for enemy people.[4] Billy Sunday showed just how supreme Christ was over Caesar when he urged his audience to enlist during World War I with these words: "The man who breaks all the rules but at last dies fighting in the trenches is better than you godforsaken mutts who won't enlist."[5] Indeed, the church has served as an important government agent in perpetuating war, providing an especially crucial role in arching war with a moral rationale. As George Marsden sums it up nicely, "The nation has set the agenda and Christians have supplied the flags and crosses."[6] Indeed, the Christian faith has been used by the political establishment because American Christians have abandoned the altar of their traditions to kneel at the throne, and tanks, of the nation.

The Idol of Economics

If the favorite East/West conflicts are primarily matters of idolatries of nation and of competing civil and public religions, favorite North/South conflicts are primarily matters of economics and idolatries of materialisms. Just as the silversmith Demetrius, the ringleader of the riot, plays the most prominent part in the biblical drama, so the economics of temple worship and emperor worship play a most important role in the saga of war. In short, economics is the ringleader of the arms race.

Ephesus was a city known for its riches, its splendor, its schools, its cosmopolitanism. A catalogue of imperial trade, much of which passed through Ephesus at this time, can be found in Revelation 18:11-13.

> The merchants of the earth also will weep and mourn for her, because no one any longer buys their cargoes, cargoes of gold and silver, jewels and pearls, cloths of purple and scarlet, silks and fine linens; all kinds of scented woods, ivories, and every sort of thing made of costly woods, bronze, iron, or marble; cinnamon and spice, incense, perfumes and frankincense; wine, oil, flour and wheat, sheep and cattle, horses, chariots, slaves, and the lives of men.

It was the Ephesian way, with its high standard of living and low-level life, that was being jeopardized by Paul's preaching

93

against idolatry. During the Artemisian festival, the city was thronged with visitors who took back with them cheap terra-cotta trinkets or expensive marble, silver, or gold statuettes as sacred souvenirs of their visit. It was a profitable business, trafficking in these amulets and shrines, most of which were probably votive images of the goddess, models of the temple, or incense burners shaped like altars. Demetrius rallied both the skilled craftsmen (verse 24) and unskilled laborers (verse 25), not merely because a depressed shrine market, caused by Paul's preaching, meant that money would be stripped from their pockets. The masses were not going to be moved by jewelers going out of business or vested class interests being attacked. But they could be moved by appeals to civic pride (we're no longer Number One) and religious prejudice (our deities are being maligned). By shrewdly combining economic self-interest, which got the Ephesians' attention, with patriotism and religious devotion, Demetrius was able to organize a protest demonstration against Paul, which turned into a mass demonstration against the Christians, which turned into a mindless riot.

The key word here was business. It still is. The American way of life, defined in quantitative rather than qualitative terms, is as much an idol as the Ephesian way of life. The lengths a society more devoted to profits than people will go to in accommodating itself to the atomic age is revealed in southern Nevada's adjustment to nuclear weapons testing in its backyard during the 1950s. Beauty parlors advertised "atomic hairdos," bars mixed up "atomic cocktails," promoters sponsored at Sands Hotel a "Miss Atom Bomb" contest, bands played the boogie-woogie "Atom Bomb Bounce," and one enterprising investor put money into the "Atomic View Motel," where guests were promised they could watch atomic flashes from lounge chairs.[7] In the East, philosophical materialism persecutes Christians. In the West, practical materialism seduces Christians.

Erich Fromm, in one of his German radio broadcasts, described this materialistic form of idolatry as "a new religion" for the twentieth century. He called it the "religion of technology."[8] There are many forms of this new religion. One is faith in technology as the solution to every problem, a notion that first turned scientists and artists like Archimedes, Leonardo da Vinci, and Michelangelo into virtual arms merchants, and later seduced modern scientists like J. Robert Oppenheimer, Rudolf Peierls, Enrico Fermi, Leo Szilard, Sir Frank Whittle, Sir John Randall, Henry Albert Howard Boot, and Charles Stark Draper into admitting the military into their laboratories, at some stage in their careers. Many of these scientists later repented of their complicity in war research. Leo Szilard, the nuclear scientist who campaigned hard for nuclear disarmament, took particular delight in the story of Willard Libby, a 1961 commissioner on the Atomic Energy Commission. In an attempt to demonstrate how the most elementary technology could help anyone survive a nuclear war, Libby built a bomb shelter out of sandbags and railroad ties at a cost of only thirty dollars. A few weeks after it was built, a neighborhood brush fire completely wiped it out. "This proves not only that there is a God," Szilard observed, "but that God has a sense of humor."

But while scientists like Szilard, Oppenheimer, and others have publicly renounced their cooption by the military, they have not seen their deeper cooption by the pagan deity of technology itself. Toward the end of World War I, Orville Wright said, "When my brother and I built the first man-carrying machine, we thought that we were introducing into the world an invention that would make further war practically impossible."[9] Similar hopes animated Alfred Nobel, the inventor of dynamite, who set out to create, in his words, "a substance or machine with such terrible power of mass destruction that war would thereby be made impossible forever."[10] Such notions would elicit our pity if there were not such a strong possibility that pity could explode in our faces. That kind of fiction feeds on itself like a malignant tumor, until it eats everything away, leaving an empty soul and a bony, bloodless, emaciated body. In spite of every evidence that technology makes war not impossible but more possible, we continue to subscribe to a Tinkerbell faith in it. In a private conversation, one of America's most informed politicians confided: "America cannot keep up with the Soviet Union's military build-up. The best we can hope for is divine intervention. I believe God is going to intervene and protect his chosen nation from the Russians by blessing America with some incredible technological breakthrough that will render nuclear weapons obsolete." You have to rub your eyes to believe it. It is enough to make even an atheist lose faith.

To solve the problems of technology's idolatry by applying more technology is to make a horror into a habit. It is the equivalent of Satan's rebuking sin. It is as unlikely to succeed as charging mortgage payments to one's credit card. One problem only compounds the other. To offer but one example of this, a "computopian faith" (Cees J. Hamelink), which gives technology a life of its own, may make Judgment Day more inevitable if not immediate. Technology's newest know-it-all, the computer, cannot be programmed without error. America's famous "launch alerts" of 1979–80, caused by "computer malfunction," demonstrated that technology is not "fail-safe." NORAD had near-misses in 1960, 1971, and 1979; the Polaris nuclear missile submarine had a near-miss in 1971. Even if one estimates the probability of an "accidental" nuclear war at less than 5 percent (generous, given computer operators' notoriously low reliability), accidental nuclear war becomes a virtual certainty within the next one hundred years. For Christians to trust in ancient gods to save them—military redeemers the Pentagon has named "Jupiter" (intermediate-range ballistic missile of the late fifties), "Thor" (an early sixties missile with a fifteen-hundred-mile range), "Atlas" (the Air Force's first intercontinental ballistic missile), "Volkire" (the experimental strategic bomber XB70), "Poseidon" (the first nuclear powered submarine), and its successor, "Trident" (both armed with missiles of the same name)—is to play Judas to Jesus.

The twinkling theologizing of technological faith was never made brighter to me than when I went on an official tour of the armed forces in December of 1986, designed to increase awareness among civic leaders of the military's "mission." I decided to accept the Air Force's invitation partly because I was working on this book and partly because I had just finished rereading Émile Durkheim's last great work, *The Elementary Forms of the Religious Life* (1915), wherein he argued that a society for which its people are unwilling to die cannot long survive. Probably never again would I have a better opportunity to get to know the mind of the military, I thought, and to explore those American values and traditions for which so many of our men and women were willing to die.

On the long plane trip to Edwards Air Force Base in California, I struck up a lengthy, at times pastoral, conversation with the commander of Wright-Patterson Air Force Base in Dayton. I found General Charles Fox to be a devout Christian, deeply concerned about the plight of the church and the condition of lost souls. I mentioned to him that I was writing this book and introduced him to civil/public religion's concept of two-timing Christians, where country competes with God for religious devotion. I then asked him how much of a problem he thought the idolatry of nation presented to him personally and to military personnel in general. "We don't have that problem," he responded quickly and, as I thought at the time, too glibly. "If anything, there's not enough emphasis on love for one's country in the military. There's not enough attention given to what this country stands for."

THE LION'S PRIDE

As astonishing as it seems, and no one is more astounded than I, by the time I left Edwards' three hundred thousand square acres of desert tumbleweed and Joshua trees, I had come to agree with him. I expected to find in the military mind a patriotic fervor that cradled the Bible in the flag and immersed both in the baptismal waters of democracy, freedom, and liberty. But instead of "rah-rah America," what I heard was "gee-whiz technology." We are the nation that put people on the moon, and the nation that put people on the moon can surely put the best fighter planes in the sky. Uppermost in the hearts of the men and women I encountered was pride in the wizardry of America's weapons and in the marriage of the military to space-age technology. Could it be, I mused silently, that Americans are still willing to die for the American way of life, but a life now defined less in terms of freedom, democracy, liberty, and equality than in terms of technological supremacy and superior weaponry? Is not this shift in what we are willing to die for confirmed by what we have become in the world: the world's largest exporter, not of wonder-working values, but of wonder-working weapons? Is this not what we are best known for, and what our military is understandably proudest of—being the nation with the most razzle-dazzle weaponry, the most magical technology?

The religion of technology has such strong appeal, and technology is such a demanding idol, because it promises to make us into God, if only we will allow technology to do whatever it can, which is the chief ethical principle of technological piety. That is why technology ultimately causes us to bow down rather than boast. Technology provides us with more than "immediate gratification." All our multiplying needs can be met and "totally gratified." Technology makes us all escapees, slipping the chains of work and effort, freeing us to be the rulers of paradise we were intended to be.

But humans end up as machines in a technological

98

millennium, bearing and becoming the image of what they have made. As the psalmist describes the process (115:5-8):

> [Idols] have mouths that cannot speak,
>   and eyes that cannot see;
> they have ears that cannot hear,
>   nostrils, and cannot smell;
> with their hands they cannot feel,
>   with their feet they cannot walk,
>   and no sound comes from their throats.
> Their makers grow to be like them,
>   and so do all who trust in them.

The most powerful moment in *Jesus Christ Superstar*, for me, was the Temple scene, when buyers and sellers actually became the shapes of the things they bought and sold.

I have two vivid memories of this Air Force trip, which will etch on my mind forever the welding of humanity and technology; they occurred while I was inspecting the experimental prototype AFTI-F16, and our country's chief fighter plane, the F16. Since cameras were not permitted, questions from our group seemed freer. Someone asked when fighter pilots were permitted to switch to manual and truly fly the plane. Our host explained patiently that there are no manual overrides in today's jets. In other words, humans no longer can bring these machines under their own control, for there is nothing there to control. Everything is electronics and information processing. The pilot is literally sitting at the seat of the world's most advanced and deadly computer video game. Later, when I climbed into the wraparound cockpit of an F16, heard the glass bubble lock in place, and realized that this plane could talk to the pilot and recognize his voice, I felt as if I were literally wearing the cockpit—a cyborg in space. The plane and I were married, as much as any husband and wife.

The military's near apotheosis of astronauts is surprising only in its fervor, for it reflects the emerging role of astronauts in our culture as the "high priests" of this religion of the "right stuff." The priests-in-training even looked like Greek gods, every pilot having passed some Adonis look-alike test. The commander of the Air Force's Tactical Training Wing, which sires these perfect human specimens, had many religious things to say about their mission, including incantational mantras like "Lose Sight, Lose Fight" and theological reminders that for every F15 or F16 fighter pilot, there are seventeen support people keeping the pilot in the air. Erich Fromm contends that the "spectacle and the enthusiasm" with which Americans observed the astronauts' landing on the moon in 1969 "had the quality of a pagan religious ceremony."[11] A worshiping America froze in absolute disbelief, as their priests and prophets died fifty-seven seconds after the lift-off of Challenger 7. The belief that technology had made humans capable of transcending human limitations, even the "surly bonds of earth," to become like God, was hushed; the god of technology had been temporarily silenced.

The Idol of Crowd-Pleasing

We want to be liked; we need to have people pamper and pet us with words of affection and praise. This is the "Spaniel Syndrome," an idolatry of popularity which afflicts the church today as much if not more than it afflicted the Jews in Luke's story of the Ephesian riot. The mob rushed into the city's amphitheater, the place where the games were held and public meetings took place. Whipped into a wild state of frenzy, especially by the religious appeal which always carried the crowd, the mob had become mindlessly mad. Serge Moscovici's *The Age of the Crowd* establishes as the basic principle of crowd psychology that individuals making up a crowd are less intelligent and creative than when they are alone.[12] But here was a mob so crazed with hatred that many could not remember the reason for the riot in the first place.

Or as Luke put it contemptuously, "most of them did not know what they had all come for" (Acts 19:32). The sound of the mob must have been truly frightening, enough so that this incident may have been what Paul had in mind when he wrote, "I 'fought wild beasts' at Ephesus" (I Corinthians 15:32). Indeed, we are told that spectators watching beasts tear apart slaves in the circus amphitheater at Hippo rent the air with shrieks louder than the yells of soldiers defending the city gates from invaders.

Ephesian Jews, widely known for hating idols, were afraid that the uproar might turn into a riot against the Jews as well as against the Christians, because of Paul's ethnic background. To defend themselves, they selected Alexander as their sweet-talking spokesperson, perhaps the same Alexander who was the coppersmith named in II Timothy as an enemy of Paul (4:14). Standing before the screaming throng, Alexander tried to please and appease the crowd by dissociating himself from Paul and the Jews from the Christians. But playing to the galleries often backfires. The sight of a Jew, and thus not an Artemis worshiper, further enraged the mob. For two hours they screamed hysterically, chanting the rhythmical, cultic cry,

> Me-ga-le-hē Ar-te-mis Ephesiōn
> (Great is Artemis of the Ephesians)
>
> Me-ga-le-hē Ar-te-mis Ephesiōn
> (Great is Artemis of the Ephesians)

Luke's lyrical description of this phenomenon ("A voice came as one out of all") should not temper our sense of the hatred felt by the Roman world for the Jews, and its resentment of this Christian sect for not trafficking in, but indeed attacking, its idols. The more people cry "Peace! Peace!" the more we know there is no peace. The louder and longer the crowd howled "Me-ga-le-hē Ar-te-mis, Me-ga-le-hē Ar-te-mis" the more it testified to the fading away of Artemis' greatness and the successful inroads made by Paul and these early Christians into the hearts of the people.

Jesus had a peculiar view of crowds and victims, violence and oppression. He did not pity the one who is struck; he pitied those who strike. Jesus taught us to expect to "be struck" as a matter of course. That is why William James' observation that the trouble with Christians is that they are forever lobbying for special favors in the courts of the Almighty is so damning. That is why the idol of crowd-pleasing is such an offense. It inevitably turns the gospel, not the world, upside down. If Christians have not already discovered that, as novelist Vladimir Nabokov said in a television interview, "it's a short walk from the hallelujah to the hoot," then an idol has been made of popularity. To be a disciple is to take that short walk frequently. To be a Christian in today's pagan culture is to confront angry crowds.

Better than anyone, pastors should know from experience the sounds of howling mobs, for they are called to be in the frontlines and trenches, smashing idols. It should not be surprising to find both crowds and individuals with ravenous appetites for roasted clergy. What is surprising is the lengths to which clergy will go, like Alexander, to redirect hungers they themselves have aroused, efforts which end up only intensifying natural desires. People who are not stirred up are people who have not had their idols smashed. And in America today, there are far too few incidents of howling mobs. At least in "godless communism" society takes the church seriously enough to persecute it.

Some of the bad habits clergy have developed in crowd-pleasing include being charitable about everyone, being studiously inoffensive, and giving what G. K. Chesterton called "easy speeches that comfort cruel men"—the habit of leaning not so much to the right or to the left as with the wind. We profess to join Paul (I Corinthians 9:22 RSV) in becoming "all things to all [people]" in order to win them to Christ. But we really become all things to all people because we like it that way. Isn't that the real reason why we stay there and move in with them? Isn't that why we now sing "Stop the World—I Want to Get On"? The prayer of the ancient Pharisee used to be: "God, I thank thee that I am not like other [people]" (Luke 18:11 RSV). The prayer of the modern Pharisee now is: "I thank thee, God, that I am like other people."

To join the forces of conformist, crowd-pleasing religion is to leave the camp of light for the camp of darkness. The basest of professions, Plato believed, were those whose stock-in-trade was flattery—and preachers can rank right up there with beauticians and courtiers. Luke 6:26 is the key verse: "Alas for you when all speak well of you." John Wesley took this verse very seriously and tried to ferret out what in today's terms could be called yo-yo preachers, who allowed themselves to be manipulated by all sorts of jerks. When he visited the various Methodist societies, he customarily charged them with this question: "Who has your pastor made angry with him this past year?" If the names of specific individuals were not forthcoming, John Wesley disciplined that preacher. The early Methodist itinerant Freeborn Garrettson believed that "obedience to God is better than the smiles of friends or foes."[13] Peter Cartwright used to speak of worthless, crowd-pleasing preachers as limpy lettuce under a shadetree.[14]

Clergy are in the ministry to sometimes have a bad time. If clergy are preaching more than sweet, creamy, chocolate-box convictions, not everyone will like them. Not everyone will crave them. Jesus warned, "You will be hated by all for my name's sake" (Matthew 10:22 RSV). The same goes for the laity. In a sermon, "The Feast of Stephen," Kenneth Arnold reminds us that the church's first martyr was a layperson, a finance chairperson called to keep the books, not to staff the front lines. In the church, everybody gets stoned.[15]

It is not good for a Christian to be, nor has Jesus promised that we would be, carried to heaven on "flowery beds of ease." We don't need to go to the other extreme of thinking that we are called to be transported on beds of nails, either. But a life of challenges, obstacles, and collective struggle brings out the best in the faith. Like captured herring who remain alive during transport to market because the North Sea fishermen put enemy fish in their tanks, the church is kept alive by the struggle against idolatries. Every sheepfold needs some wolves. Even eternity, William Blake asserts at the end of *The Four Zoas* (1797), will have its own form of conflict and wolves. He calls it "intellectual war."

It is easy to play Devil's advocate. It is excruciating to commit oneself to a position. It is painful to have standards like that O'Hare Airport shoeshine man who looked at my discount-store shoes, shook his head, and waved me away with "I have my standards." The church has too many Devil's advocates already; it needs more God's advocates. I tell seminarians that unless they shuck the ball and chain of popularity, unless they have faith in God enough to

> Dare to be a Daniel,
> Dare to stand alone!
> Dare to have a purpose firm!
> Dare to make it known!
> ("Daniel's Band," Philip Bliss)

they should not go into the ministry. There are more honest ways to make a living—like stealing, arson, hijacking, and pimping. Being despised and rejected won't make your day. But it may make your life.

The Idol of Politics

There is no more misunderstood figure in the story of the Ephesian riot than that of the city official, the equivalent of today's mayor, who addresses the crowd, settles them down, and sends them home. One of the little mysteries in nearly two millennia of biblical interpretation is the almost universal celebration of this public figure for saving Paul's life. Why did the mayor not step in right away and sober the crowd? His speech tells why.

Like every good politician, he researched the problem, waited until all the right information had come in, and then acted. It is a beautiful, shrewd, and powerful speech, a model of brilliant argumentation encased in carefully picked and packed phrases. You are shouting to prove something no one has denied, the mayor pointed out to the crowd. These Christians are not guilty of sacrilege (verse 37); there has been no report of criminal activity (verses 38, 40). In fact, Demetrius and his fellow guild members have not brought forth one shred of evidence against these Christians, nor officially charged them with anything. No one seriously disputes that what you are shouting is true. Artemis *is* great. Thus there is no need to worry. In fact, no one is in danger here but us, for we have not acted as Greek citizens but as barbarians.

In many ways, don't fear Artemis. Don't fear Ephesus. Don't fear Demetrius. Don't fear Alexander. Don't even fear the howling mob. Fear the mayor, and all those who would idolize the political way out of conflict, which seeks peace at any price. In spite of the outcome, the mayor was not a friend of the Christians. If there had been a violent riot in Ephesus, Rome would know why. Rome would hold the magistrates responsible, and they would have lost their jobs. The mayor saved Paul and his companions, but only because he was saving himself first. John Calvin is one of the few commentators on this passage to see the mayor for what he was—a master politician. It was his political savvy that led him to "calm the excited crowd by any means whatever. . . . For the sake of putting a stop to the strife, he extols the spurious divinity of Diana, and affirms her superstitious cult."[16]

The state proved to be the Christians' best defense against mob violence, the reliable defender of public order. But the cost was high: the establishment of a sham shalom, or what Gustavo Gutierrez calls a "liar society," where peace is called for but greed is what is kept (Jeremiah 6:13-14; 8:11). The idolatry of politics resides in the great assumption that political means can solve and heal problems. It is only a small step from advocating political action to taking violent action, because one has already accepted the premise that whatever works is right: peace at any price. The patronage of all political idols, especially the state, offers peace, but peace on its own terms. Politics is a master at peacekeeping, and the United Nations' "peacekeeping forces" rightly named. But what is needed most is peacemaking. As Paul and his companions discovered, politics has something significant to offer the church: the peace that the world gives. But politics offers cut-price peacemaking, the feeling of being at peace without seriously challenging the premises and idols of war. The kind of peace that the world gives depends on what part of the world gets to give the peace—and each part is self-serving, smug, and false. If God does not establish peace, there can be no peace.

And there was no peace at Ephesus, only the mirage of peace. There also was no peace for Paul, who escaped (but just barely) with his life. John Calvin sets the stage for why Paul was cast into such a great depression after leaving Ephesus. "If Paul had been in the theatre at that moment [when the mayor defended the goddess Artemis] he would have exposed himself to death a hundred times, rather than allow himself to be rescued at this price."[17] All of Paul's efforts were dismissed when that crowd dispersed, and he left Ephesus terribly distraught. In Paul's own words, which one even trembles to type: "We do not want you to be uninformed . . . about the hardships we suffered in the province of Asia. We were under great pressure, far beyond our ability to endure, so that we despaired even of life" (II Corinthians 1:8-9 NIV).

There is one more idol we must look at. It is the idol that brought Paul, in his own words, to the brink of death.

The Idol of Security

The Asiarchs were the wealthiest and most aristocratic inhabitants of the province. They were in charge of public affairs in Asia, including the worship of Caesar. For reasons we are not sure of, some Asiarchs were friends of Paul. Christians may, like Paul, have friends in high places. These friends cared deeply about Paul's safety and tried to protect him. Paul wanted to face the mob. Sometimes this is the right thing to do; sometimes it is not. The Asiarchs were convinced that the mob's threat to Paul's life was serious and that he had too much yet to do to throw his life away at this point by going to the stadium. Paul succumbed to the pressure from his friends and their concern about his security. He left Ephesus without setting foot in the stadium. But he repented of this decision the rest of his life. It was the one time in his life as a disciple of Jesus Christ that he could not say "I have fought a good fight. I have kept the faith."

The Asiarchs were in many ways like the rich young man of Matthew 19:16-22, who was a prototype of modern Americans. He was a caring, loving, giving person. He wanted to do what was right with his life and to live a life pleasing in God's sight. He had high moral principles and served his family and community with faithfulness and integrity. He wanted to use his wealth to help the poor. But when Jesus asked him to be without life insurance, which protects from the insecurities of death, to be without a pension program, which protects from the insecurities of aging, to be without health plans, which protect from the insecurities of disease, to be without savings accounts, which protect from the insecurities of emergencies—when Jesus asked him to risk living without job security, financial security, social security, national security, or even personal security, and to follow him, the young man's deepest idol was threatened, and he went sadly away.

The word "security" comes from the combination of a Latin prefix and a Latin word: *se* means "without" and *cure* is "care." Without care. What do we want most from life? Security, to be without care about our personal future and fulfillment. What does the nation want most in the world? Security, to be without care about its safety and destiny. Like the young man in Matthew, we think such security comes through seeking security, strength through building up strength. The "transcending goal" of our defense establishment, declares the fifth edition of the Pentagon's influential *Soviet Military Power* (1986), is "peace and security." What does the Pentagon mean by "security"? *The Dictionary of Military and Associated Terms,* published by the Joint Chiefs of Staff, defines "national security" as a condition of "military or defense advantage over any foreign nation or group of nations." More weapons, in other words, buy more security. Peace can be found under the umbrella security of the mushroom cloud.

Not only has security become an idol, but the idol has become more and more the image of armaments. The first "thou-shalt-have-no-other-gods-before-me" commandment was said by Martin Luther (*The Small Catechism,* 1529) to mean "we should fear, love, and trust in God above all things." Jörg Zink updates Luther's commentary: "Today we fear the Russians above all things, we love our possessions above all else, and we trust superior military potential above all things."[18] The biblical passage often quoted to support this position is Luke 11:21 (RSV): "When a strong man, fully armed, guards his own palace, his goods are in peace." But if one reads the next verse, one discovers that the point being stressed is the opposite one—not the security of arms but their insecurity: "But when one stronger than he assails him and overcomes him, he takes away his armor in which he trusted, and divides his spoil." The security of arsenals of hatred yields what Ira Chernus calls in *Dr. Strangegod* "spiraling insecurity,"[19] for there is always someone, someday, who can match your weapon with an even more destructve weapon,[20] gun for gun, bomb for bomb, missile for missile. The security of the "Star Wars" Strategic Defense Initiatives is no different from the security purchased by the sixteen-hundred-mile Great Wall of China, built in the third century before Christ, or the Maginot Line built by France in this century. Somebody will always come along with an invention that can scale your wall, penetrate your forts, or crack your dome, no matter how invincible each appears at the time.

In being more concerned at Ephesus about his own security and safety than the security and safety of the gospel, Paul is presented as contradicting his own testimony laid out in II Corinthians 12:10 (NKJV). "I take pleasure in infirmities, in reproaches, in needs, in persecutions, in distresses, for Christ's sake. For when I am weak, then I am strong." What kind of double-talk discipleship is this: "When I am weak, then I am strong"; when I risk insecurities, then I find my greatest security?

Paul's point on "weakness," or what John Howard Yoder calls "the weight of weakness" and "servant strength,"[21] is related to his notion of sustaining divine grace. His weakness itself adds nothing. But it is the very thing that necessitates God's intervention. Paul differs from all others not because his weakness is so pronounced that it somehow equals or becomes strength. Rather, Paul perceives the truth that not he, but God, is strong. As Paul gives himself in service, as he dares doing that which he is inherently incapable of, precisely then he knows God's sustaining, powerful grace, which is perfected in weakness. This theological paradox lies behind Paul's statement and allows him to differentiate between himself and God—unlike many electronic evangelists, who mistake the voice of exigency for the voice of divinity.

Second, Paul's double-talk is a deductive recognition that no person, no nation, can make life secure. One can only live life fully by accepting all its insecurities. No one ever learned to walk, or swim, or ride a bike, clutching the idol of security. No one ever fell in love without blowing the idol of security to smithereens. One cannot simultaneously have security and love, or anything else good in life.

Ironically, our defense establishment has discovered all by itself the security of insecurity. The X29, popularly known as the airplane with its wings on backward, is America's prototype jet fighter of tomorrow. Scientists have deliberately created a plane that is 35 percent unstable, so unstable in fact that without digital electronics the plane would rip itself apart in microseconds. Why has our military built a plane so unstable and feeble of frame? The instability increases many times over the plane's efficiency, control, maneuverability, and power. The X29 is able to do things no plane has ever done before, things never even conceived as possible in the air, precisely because of its daring instability and feebleness.

At Ephesus, Paul lost an opportunity to do something great for God, because he wanted both to preserve his security and to promote the gospel. But the gospel could be proclaimed only at the high cost of insecurity. We know from hindsight that Paul's life was not nearly as in danger as the Asiarchs thought. For one thing, once the ringleader Demetrius got much of the city to the assembly, he disappeared from the scene and was no longer an actor in the drama. The least harmful demagogues are those good at starting trouble and stirring up a mob but lousy at knowing what to do with all that wound-up energy. For another thing, after venting its rage for two hours, the crowd was ready to listen. As the Mayor's appearance and address revealed, the crowd then could be swayed by skillful reason and smooth rhetoric.

Jesus asks us, as he asked that rich young man, for our entire paycheck. There is no clearer statement in the Bible of the danger of idols or the cost of being the "people of Yahweh" than the Hebrew tradition of the ban, which required warriors to refrain from claiming or acquiring any profit from fighting in Yahweh's war.

Yahweh instructed the Israelites never to "plunder the Egyptians" or take their "spoil," for when they did they would create a golden calf. This was the basic principle behind the *herem* holy war, where the enemies' *herem* or "devoted things" (e.g., Joshua 6:18 RSV) were not to be picked up. The point of the *herem* restrictions was not the annihilation of the enemy, but the preservation of Israel's identity, holiness, and faithfulness to Yahweh. How different this God is from today's *Oh, God* God—friendly, casual, wisecracking, harmless. The mind almost remembereth not to the contrary.

Herem's warnings against the world's "devoted things" are at best dismissed nowadays as so much threshing of old theological straw. Indeed, "plundering the Egyptians" has become something of which the church is proud—its increase in wealth, power, and prestige (our golden calf industry) has become big business. Christians today are surrounded by a paganism that is similar to that which the early church had to contend with.[22] The idols of religion, nation, economics, politics, and security are such a part of everyday existence and payday life-styles that the church can make little progress in peacemaking until it cleaves closer to the covenant.

The processes of weaning away and weeding out idolatries must be undertaken in earnest. Like the Christians at Thessalonica praised by Paul, the church must insist that people who become "converted to God" and "servants of the living and true God" have indeed "broke[n] with the worship of false gods" (I Thessalonians 1:9 NJB). Like the Christians at Colossia, the church must make sure that no one deprives us of freedom by some secondhand, empty, rational philosophy based on the principles of this world instead of on Christ (Colossians 2:8). The church must also be prepared to face the consequences of being socially disruptive of those "principalities and powers" (Colossians 2:15 RSV) that contend for primacy with Jesus Christ. Every Sunday morning the worshiping church should serve as a mass demonstration and protest against the coliseums of the world and the idolatries of a pagan culture. The church should be prone to deliberate acts of provocation, set to upset the established order.

This will entail courage. Sometimes it will entail stalking tigers in the "mud and blood" of the way of the cross. But crucifixion is the biggest tiger trap of all.

CHAPTER 5

The Lion of Judah and Lion-Tamers

> If the Tiber rises as high as the city walls, if the Nile does not
> rise to the fields, if the weather will not change, if there is an
> earthquake, a famine, a plague—straightway the cry is heard:
> "Toss the Christians to the lion!" So many of them for just one
> beast?
>
> —Tertullian, *Apology*

The church's domain is the kingdom of lions, messianic
emblems of strength, courage, piety, intellectual prowess,
and God's power (Genesis 49:9). But lions that run free,
roaming Palestine in the joy and splendor of their kingdom,
are now an endangered species. Most lions are living in
captivity, caged spectacles in circuses where lion-tamers strut
their majesty and mastery over lions. The grandstands know
that the lion is stronger than the lion-tamer. So does the
lion-tamer. The key is that the lion doesn't know. What if
Christians helped lions awaken to their character and
pedigree?

Peacemaking is supposed to be one of the distinguishing
characteristics of Jews and Christians. The Jews of the first
century referred to peace-loving, peacemaking people as
"sons of Aaron": children of peace. God is called in the Bible
"the God of Peace." Jesus is called "the Prince of Peace." The
Holy Spirit is called "the Spirit of Peace." "Peace" is how the
early Christians greeted each other. Paul even gave a higher
priority to peace than he did to the institution of marriage (I
Corinthians 7:15).

113

One of the earliest Christian slogans said, "We are the race given over to peace." We are more than a race of *Homo sapiens*, less than the sum of our parts, when we are merely *Homo Novus* (1917), *Homo Ludens* (Johan Huizinga, 1938), *Homo Viator* (Gabriel Marcel, 1944), *Homo Faber* (Max Frisch, 1957), *Homo Religiosus* (Giorgio Zunini, 1966), *Homo Spiritualis* (Steven E. Ozment, 1969), *Homo Futurus* (Vera Graaf, 1971), *Homo Loquens* (Dennis Fry, 1977), and *Homo Quaerens* (Leonard Charles Feldstein, 1978). We are also called to be a race of *Homo pacis*—a people of peace, a people who *know war no more*. Ever since the appearance of the first *Homo sapiens* forty thousand years ago, *Homo's* inexpressible gift for warfare seems to have had the upper hand while *pacis* has been in eclipse. But the hope for *Homo sapiens* is in *Homo pacis*.

Unlike the solitary tiger, lions are sociable beings. These plain-colored large cats live in family groups called prides, in which they hunt, play, and preside over the animal kingdom. The mandate of the New Testament for the daughters and sons of Aaron is clear: The follower of Jesus is to be a peacemaker, one who points the way to a world where the hawk and the dove, the sheep and the wolf, the tiger and the turkey, the eagle and the bear cohabit in the lion's pride. The highest praise a Christian can receive today is the praise Josephus reserved for Ananus, of whom he wrote: "Above all, he desired to make peace."[1]

Wesley Yoakum tells of an evening several years ago when, after the children were supposedly put to bed for the night, he headed for the seclusion of his study while his wife, Jerri, changed into an oversized sweatshirt and an old pair of jeans and proceeded to wash her hair. She suddenly became aware that the children were not sleeping, and as the noise from their bedroom became louder and wilder, she decided something needed to be done. So, finishing her shampoo as quickly as she could, she wrapped a large turkish towel around her head, stormed into the bedroom, and put them both back into bed with a stern warning to stay there and be quiet. Sensing something was amiss, Wes emerged from his study in time to overhear two-year-old Chad ask his older brother in a trembling voice, "Who was that?"

Who has not had a similar reaction to some who are running around crying "Peace, peace," when there is no peace. Who has not wondered, Who was that? when Christians poured blood on draft files, latched themselves to missiles, or climbed over military base fences into the waiting arms of the police. Who are these people who call themselves "peacemakers"? What can we say about those who pursue peace by protesting war?

This question of identity, "who was that?" looms so large because the world is in desperate need of *Homo pacis:* a people who say, "We are the race given over to peace." If you let children play with dangerous instruments, it won't be long before there is a hideous accident. No one in the church wants an accident with nuclear toys to happen. When it comes to nuclear war, everyone is a pacifist. Everyone in the church says: "I'm against war. I'm for peace." But the question is, *How?* We all know where we should be. But we all disagree on a peace plan, on how to get there from here. We are like the teenager whose mother picked her up at high school to take her to the dentist. All the way to the dentist's office the girl chattered excitedly about an English placement test that she had taken which revealed that she was in the top 8 percent in the nation in "the ability to understand sentences and to give meanings to words." She was also in the top 3 percent in her ability "to understand direct statements and to perceive the motive and ideas behind them." She rambled on and on about her high scores. The mother said that when they arrived at the dentist's office, there was a big sign on the door that read "PULL"—and her daughter pushed, and the dental work had to be postponed on account of a swollen lip.

We've read the Bible, we've heard the sermons, we've

entered into the litanies for peace, we've studied the church's documents on peace. Theologically, we're in the top 3 percent. But when it comes right down to getting into the dentist's office, we can't tell the difference between push and pull.

Albert Camus once wrote that when one has no character one has to apply a method. One of the reasons the church has been so preoccupied with method in recent years is that we have not adequately emphasized the importance of character. We have forgotten that ethics relates to character as well as conduct. We have been so enamored of an ethics of doing that an ethics of being, which raises critical questions of identity, values, and attitudes, has largely been forgotten. Isn't it true that if someone says "she has character" or "he has character," it usually means they think she, or he, has a difficult character? Aren't those the kinds of people you think of when you recollect the "character builders" of your past? My favorite portion of Charles G. Finney's *Lectures on Revivals of Religion,* written in 1835 by the father of modern revivalism and one of the most important figures in the nineteenth century, is an itemization of the "Consequences of Having the Spirit."

Five of them are as follows:

1. You will be called eccentric; and probably you will deserve it. Probably you will really be eccentric. I never knew a person who was filled with the spirit, that was not called eccentric. And the reason is, that they are unlike other people. . . .

2. . . . It is not unlikely you will be thought deranged, by many. We judge men to be deranged, when they act differently from what we think to be prudent and according to common sense, and when they come to conclusions for which we can see no good reasons. . . .

3. . . . You must expect to feel great distress in view of the church and the world. Some spiritual epicures ask for the spirit because they think it will make them so perfectly

happy. Some people think that spiritual Christians are always very happy and free from sorrow. There never was a greater mistake. . . .

4. You will be often grieved with the state of the ministry. . . . Christians do often get spiritual views of things, and their souls are kindled up, and then they find that their minister does not enter into their feelings, that he is far below the standard of what he ought to be, and in spirituality far below some of the members of his church. . . .

5. . . . You must make up your mind to have much opposition, both in the church and the world. Very likely the leading men in the church will oppose you.[2]

But in order to *be* a peacemaker, you need the *being* of a peacemaker. You need a distinctive character. You need special ways of reacting and behaving. If we are creatures of habit, as psychologists say we are, then we had better make sure we cultivate habits that make us peacemaking creatures. One of the most essential of the "things that make for peace," as Jesus put it, are *people* that make for peace: "*Blessed* are the peacemakers." Below is a biblical profile of the character of a peacemaker—the kind of character powerful enough to throw a lambchop past a lion.

First, a peacemaker is a *patriot*. Patriotism is rooted in the Spanish notion of *queréncia:* affection for the place one calls home and the sense of peace and fulfillment that such a place offers. Jeremiah 29:7 reads, "Seek the welfare of any city to which I have carried you off, and pray to the Lord for it; on its welfare your welfare will depend." Peacemakers love their country, work for their country, pray for their country, and are not afraid to be known as patriots. One group of American prelates pointed this out sharply in an official statement: "Peacemaking must be exalted by the churches as a loyal expression of patriotism and honor."[3] We who are involved in the peace movement have made terrible blunders, either of promoting a "blame America first" mentality or of not showing patriotic commitment. We have been like the man who said to the old potbelly stove, "Come on, give me some warmth and I'll add the wood." It takes warmth to beget warmth. One has to show love for one's country if one expects one's country to show love. G. K. Chesterton said that Rome was not great before people loved her, but because people loved her she became great. Like the early Christians, we must pray for our nation, its governance, its success. What we must not do is worship the emperor, or the nation, as did the Ephesians.

There is nothing wrong in thinking of America as God's chosen nation. There is something wrong in thinking of America as God's *only* chosen nation. This is what has given patriotism a black eye and has chased many patriots into hiding. But as James Russell Lowell wrote to Henry James, "a man's love of his country may often be gauged by his disgust at it."[4] It is an expression of patriotism to criticize the Rambo spirit that is roaming this land and making our culture vulture-hungry for violence. When Frederick the Great of Prussia found a portrait of a man with whom he was having trouble hanging on a wall in a prominent position, he exclaimed, *"Niedriger hängen"*: "Hang the picture lower." We must find a place for America among the nations of the world, not in a superior position to them. It is our patriotic duty to "hang the picture lower"; we must get over this obsessive un-American desire to be the top dog, to be Number One. Lao-tzu's famed three treasures of life apply as much to nations as to individuals: "frugality, compassion, the desire not to be foremost in everything." No nation has the need, or deed, to be "foremost in everything."

Peace does not require that patriotism be destroyed. Peace is the enemy of perverted "love it or leave it" patriotism, but the friend of the true "love it and live it" variety. Patriotism provides us with roots that plant us in a specific place on this planet, so that we are not blown away. Too many of us have been floating above the ground because we have been afraid to say, "I'm proud to be an American. I love this country." By helping us see what our assumptions are, true patriotism keeps us from fanaticism. Indeed, patriotism enables us to catch the vision of internationalism. Internationalism is like language. You can't speak language in general, you have to speak a *particular* one. You can't amalgamate internationalism into one universal sentiment. Artists have seen this faster and clearer than anyone else. Those who aspire to be general end up being nothing. "Wer allgemein sein will, wird nicht," Goethe wrote; "you can't be universal without being provincial," is how Robert Frost makes the same point.[5] Or in the words of John, "For God so loved the world" that Jesus was sent not to the world in general, but to a specific people, the Jews, and a particular region, Palestine, and from Palestine and the Jews to everyone in the world.

Part of this patriotic character is the rediscovery and reconstruction of a useable past for a "nuclear age"—valorizing the great tradition from Jefferson to Wilson of building international relations, international trade, and international peace. The patriotic character lives between a great memory and great hope. We choose our ancestors, selecting some, keeping silent about others. Peacemakers refuse to let warmongers set the criterion for selection.[6] The true archetype of our patriotic tradition is not Indian-fighter Daniel Boone but Jonathan Chapman, better known as Johnny Appleseed, who befriended Native Americans and walked unarmed through America's forests and frontier. The truth of our patriotic tradition is not expressed in the words of General Israel Putnam at the Battle of Bunker Hill, June 17, 1775 ("Don't fire until you see the whites of their eyes"), but in the words of General Douglas McArthur at the end of his career: "I am a 100 percent disbeliever in war." Nor is it exemplified by the words Richard Nixon spoke during congressional impeachment proceedings, "I can go into my office and pick up the telephone, and in twenty-five minutes seventy million people will be dead," but in the words inscribed on the memorial cenotaph at Hiroshima:

> Let all the souls here rest in peace
> For we shall not repeat the evil.

The true patriotic tradition does not consist of winning the two world wars of this century. Rather it is, after winning these wars, in helping the defeated rebuild their institutions instead of taking revenge on them. Never before in history had any conquering nation so "occupied" a vanquished foe as America did Japan after the Second World War. We helped modernize their constitution; enfranchise Japanese women; promote free elections; release political prisoners; establish a representative government, free press, and labor movement; and generally set Japan in the path it is on today.

Second, peacemaking requires *imagination:* very simply, the ability to *imagine* peace in the midst of a world at war, as Stanley Hauerwas has taught us.[7] The character of peacemakers is shaped by the play of memory and imagination. In many translations, II Corinthians 5:17 reads, "if anyone is in Christ, he is a new creation," as if God's reconciling work in Christ were only personal and internal. There is another translation, however: "When anyone is united to Christ, there is a new world; the old order has gone, and a new order has already begun" (NEB). For the Christian, peace is more than the Old Testament understanding of shalom. Leviticus 26:3-13 gives a rich account of what shalom would be like. But shalom was always somewhat eschatological to the Hebrew mind. It was always a coming advent, never a current event or prospect. With the cross of Jesus Christ, peace becomes a reality. There is a whole new way of looking at things in Christ, a whole new perspective on this world that is now possible. How many Christians are living as if Jesus were coming tomorrow, when they should be living as if Jesus were here today—because he is? How many Christians are acting as if the new creation were only in the future, when they should be acting as if the new creation were here today—because it is? There is an unbroken connection between our imaginative life and our spiritual life.

"Must then a Christ perish in torment in every age to save those that have no imagination?" In the epilogue of Bernard Shaw's *St. Joan*, these famous words are spoken by Cauchon, Bishop of Beauvais, to the English chaplain who at Joan's trial had called for her burning. Now the chaplain is old, and crushed by what he has done: "I did a very cruel thing once, because I did not know what cruelty was like. I had not seen it, you know. That is the great thing: you must see it. And then you are redeemed and saved."[8]

The biggest impediment to peace is the poverty of our "moral imagination," a phrase borrowed from Edmund Burke's *Reflections on the Revolution in France* (1790), the mind-forged manacle that prevents us from seeing the vision of a world at peace, and that peace is not just some glittering, unrealizable ideal but the only reality in a world at war and a way of life already present among a community of people called Christians. Working to end evil appears about as rewarding as the legendary efforts of King Canute to turn back the waves. But war is the by-product of civilization, the militarization of power, one of the signal inventions of the first civilized tribes. Dueling, lynching, and slavery have been eliminated in a sinful world. Why not ban the bomb? Why not abolish nuclear war?

We must fight the stigma that the church, like Oxford, is the home of lost causes, the most lost of which is the cause of peace. Christians should have no interest in championing lost causes, because the resurrection finds a home in the winner's circle for every just cause. Our world is not merely a hostage to nuclear war; our minds are also hostages, our spirits held captive. "The real exile of Israel in Egypt," Martin Buber stated, quoting the Talmud, "was that they learned to endure it." The prospect of a nuclear holocaust is so vivid that it bends the imagination out of shape. Our imagination needs to be freed from the grip of broiled bodies and vaporized cities, freed from the powers of the Pentagon's imagination, where for years think tanks have been spinning the most fantastic scenarios about the future. Our problem is not a lack of imagination. The Pentagon has enough of that for everyone. It is the desperate lack of a Christian imagination that can counter obsessions with evil. The problem is the same as that of the little child who crawled out of bed after twenty minutes of trying fitfully to fall asleep, climbed into mother's and father's bed, and announced: "I came in here because there aren't any good dreams in my room." People are leaving the church and not listening to it, because the church does not have enough "good dreams" any more.

Paul the apostle says we are living between heaven and earth in the "overlap of the ages" (see I Corinthians 10:11), where the backwaters and backlash of a dying world are struggling with the birth of a new world. Peace is real. It is not a pipe dream. If it is, let the church produce more pipes. "Peace in our time" may be starry-eyed and wildly optimistic. But whose balloon is bigger? Those who believe peace is a reality, or those who argue that neither side will dare to use nuclear weapons?

In the Truman era, good, upstanding Christians like the Navy Secretary, the director of the Air War College, and Senator Stuart Symington favored dropping an atomic bomb on Russia or China, not as a defensive reaction but as an aggressive act by the United States. Neither America nor any other nation has ever refrained from using the most effective weapon it possessed at any particular time, when worse came to worse. There is no law of history or human nature that says we will not commit every atrocity the mind can conceive. Those who have faith in human ability to refrain from using what human hands have invented are not optimistic—they are deluded!

A bomb may be shaped like a cucumber, but it cannot be treated like one. Samuel Johnson said that a cucumber should be well sliced, dressed up with pepper and vinegar, and then thrown away. Every weapon that has ever been invented has been used. As Talleyrand said to Napoleon, "You can do everything with bayonets, Sire, except sit on them." Or in the words of an old Russian proverb quoted by Marshal Nikolai Ogarkov, the former Soviet Chief of Staff who issued stern warnings about the "dangerous line" we are approaching in the nuclear arms race (a man familiar to millions of Americans as the cheerful commander who explained on television the brutal shooting down of Korean Airline's Flight 007): "Even an unloaded rifle can fire once in ten years. And once in one hundred years, even a rake can produce a shot."[9] Notions of nonproliferation, or that it is possible to invent weapons and not use them, or that nuclear weapons are too horrible for anyone to dare press the button, or that there can be a "limited" nuclear war, beggar belief far more than the notion that peace is real.

You say: But we made war on poverty, and there is still poverty. The vision proved a mirage. You say: But we made war on drugs, and there are still drugs. You say: If we make war on war, won't there still be war?

The problem was not the war on poverty and drugs, but the attempt to provide material solutions to spiritual problems. This is not to say that material solutions are unimportant. In the case of peace, they have been largely untried. If we had spent as much time and money battling poverty and drugs as we did on destroying Hitler and those things that make a Hitler, things might have been different. In twelve days' time the world spends on military expenditures what it would cost to provide adequate food, water, education, health, and homes for everyone in the world for a year. We get what we pay for; we get the type of peace we pay for as well. One wonders how different the world might be if more wealthy Americans had thought like Andrew Carnegie, who gave $2 million in 1914 to establish the interreligious Church Peace Union (later renamed the Council on Religion and International Affairs). In giving the grant Carnegie said: "I have been feeling more and more that it is to the churches we must look for the bringing of peace."[10] Carnegie's imagination was so powerful that he told the group's trustees they could use the money for the eradication of poverty or other evils, should peace come to pass.

Imagination rather than imitation, then, is the second character trait of a peacemaker. Imagination means having the ability to lift anchor, free the mind from being tied up in the harbor of the old order, and sail off in the direction of the deep on the waves of the new order to which we pledge our allegiance. As Iris Murdoch has suggested, our morality is in our vision as well as in our choices. We live in our imagination. And until we are able to imagine a world without war and set people on fire with that vision of peace, we will be like the France of which Charles de Gaulle spoke when he said, she "played the part of the victim awaiting her destiny."[11] We will be like the women of the French Revolution who sat by the guillotine and counted heads as they rolled off. Belief in the inevitability of World War III becomes a self-fulfilling prophecy. In the words of physicist and biophysicist John R. Platt, "The world has become too dangerous for anything less than Utopia."[12] The world has become too dangerous for anything less than the kingdom of God.

If the second character trait allows peacemakers to lift anchor, the third lets them sail close to the wind. In other words, imagination must be followed by *ambition*. Ambition is not a dirty word for a Christian. A Christian can say both "I have ambition" and "Thine is the glory," as long as the ambition is for the things of God and God's purposes. Here is what the Bible has to say about the ambitions of a Christian: "We make it our ambition to please him [God]" (II Corinthians 5:9 NJB); "it is my ambition to bring the gospel to places where the very name of Christ has not been heard" (Romans 15:20); "let it be your ambition to keep calm and look after your own business" (I Thessalonians 4:11). Too many Christians have made it their ambition to have little ambition.

There is an old fable about some people who heard of a place called the "Cave of Truth." They discussed this among themselves and made further inquiries. Finally, they decided to set out in search of the cave, and after a long and difficult journey, they found it. At the entrance sat an old man, the guardian of the cave. They approached him and asked if indeed this was the Cave of Truth. He assured them that it was. They asked if they might enter. In reply, the guardian asked, "How deeply into the Cave of Truth do you want to go?" At this question, they retreated and talked among themselves. They returned and said, "We would like to enter and go just deep enough to say we have been there." This is what I call a Marilyn Monroe faith. Asked about her beliefs, she replied, "I just believe in everything—a little bit." Truth alone is worthy of our utter devotion and ambition.

Oscar Wilde said that the secret of life is knowing exactly how far you can go, and then going just a little bit further. This is the "and-then-some" spirit. There is a story that has been making the rounds recently about a soldier at boot camp who had been separated from his home for a long period of time. He had been getting very lonely, and his loneliness was driving him to despair. He decided he had to have an evening out, but his request was turned down. In his despair he decided to leave anyway, but as he began to leave camp a gate sentry saw him and called, "Halt." The young soldier replied: "My mother is dead and in heaven. My father is dead and in hell. My girl is alive and in New York. And I'm going to see one of them tonight." Why were the saints saints? Because they pushed on when they wanted to stand still. Because they adopted the religious equivalent of the motto of the West's railroad builders: "Ursam aut inveniam aut faciam" ("I will find a way or I will make a way"). Because they didn't sit around playing the "Ain't it awful" game; they weren't what somebody has called "awfulizers." Their ambitions led them to activity. They had the "and-then-some" spirit, the same spirit that used to prompt Senator Millard Tydings to say he would never be satisfied until his ambition was realized for all nations someday to agree on "disarmament down to rifles."

One of the least peaceful texts in the Bible is this one: "Blessed are the peacemakers, for they shall be called sons of God" (Matthew 5:9 RSV). What is so upsetting is that we would like to hear "blessed are the peaceful," or "blessed are the peace-keepers," or better yet, "blessed are the peace-lovers." But the word is not passive, it is active: "Blessed are the peace-*makers*." A pastor once said to me, "People will help you do something, but they won't help you do nothing." Even Christian pacifism is not passivism. One makes peace like one makes bread. It takes kneading and sweating and ingredients that cost money.

One of the reasons "nonviolence will not work" is that we have not spent enough money on nonviolent resources. In the Revolutionary War, it cost $.75 for every enemy killed. In the Civil War, it cost $5000 to kill a soldier; in World War I, $50,000; in World War II, $125,000. In the Vietnam War, it cost us $600,000 to kill a North Vietnamese. If there were a World War III (which would be different from all other wars because it would never be mentioned in history books), it could cost over $1 million to kill a human being. Why are people's deaths worth so much, and their lives so little? The annual financial share of the United States in the budget of the United Nations amounts to only one half of the annual budget of the Department of Sanitation of the city of New York.[13] Why is one city's garbage worth more than the world's goodwill?

THE LION OF JUDAH AND LION-TAMERS

There is a job to do. There is peace to construct. To make peace is to engage in activities that bring redemption to a broken world. Ambition is part of the character of a peacemaker, ambition to make a reality that sign found on a church bulletin board: "What a great day it will be when our daycare center has all the money it needs, and when bakesales raise money for battleships."

The fourth characteristic of a peacemaker is *patience*. In a sense we don't need to hear another sermon about the need for greater commitment to peace. We may be already doing what we can. Just last week we may have been attacked for defending our denomination's statement on peace. What we need to hear more of is the utter commitment that God has toward this whole creation. What is even more important than our commitment to God is God's commitment to us. What is infinitely more magnificent than our making peace with God, about which the New Testament has little to say, is that God has made peace a reality, *the* reality *with us.* A peacemaker knows of God's commitment to us and peace with us, and in that knowledge finds deep contentment and trust.

It is only because of that contentment that we can find the patience that peacemaking requires. Peace is not like faith, hope, and love. It does not automatically abide; it easily passes away. Patience is essential to peacemaking—patience with ourselves, patience with the church, patience with God. Not one of us can become what God wants us to be overnight. Because "we hope for what we do not see," Romans 8:25 (RSV) reads, "we wait for it with patience."

In Gerard Manley Hopkins' poem "Peace," he names patience as peace's next of kin: "And so [God] does leave Patience exquisite, that plumes to Peace thereafter."[14] Dorothee Sölle follows Hopkins in naming her collection of poetry *Die Revolutionäre Geduld (Revolutionary Patience).*[15] In China, an old parable tells of a man who went out with buckets to remove a mountain. Mountains are moved bucketfuls at a time. War is also removed bucket by bucket. The work of peace is painstaking and frustrating. Patience is indispensable.

Mark Twain loved to tell the story of the time he went to visit a friend in the country. As he walked along a narrow path he asked a farmer, "How far is it to Henderson's place?" "About a mile and a half," the farmer replied. Twain continued on for a while until he met another farmer. "How far is it to Henderson's place?" he asked again. "About a mile and a half," the second farmer answered. A while later he met still another farmer. "How far to Henderson's place?" he asked. "About a mile and a half," the third farmer answered. To which Twain replied, "Thank God I'm holding my own." Blessed are the peacemakers, for they shall never run out of work.

The final characteristic of a peacemaker is a *shalom spirituality*. It is no accident that the dove does double-duty as a symbol for both peace and the Holy Spirit. Shalom is "the central vision of world history in the Bible," Walter Brueggemann writes. The word's frequent occurrence in the Old Testament testifies to the fact that "it bears tremendous freight, the freight of a dream of God which resists all our tendencies to division, hostility, fear, drivenness and misery."[16] Spirituality is life lived in resonance with the Holy Spirit, which is not my spirit, not your spirit, but the church's spirit. Apart from God's Spirit, which makes the body of Christ come alive, "you have no power to do anything," Jesus says in his last discourse in John's Gospel. A shalom spirituality, then, is the peace of God's will. Like Piccardia in Dante's *Divine Comedy,* a shalom spirituality says, "lasua voluntate e nostra pace": "God's will is our peace." A shalom spirituality is a communal walk with God which turns one away from false gods to worship and serve the one true God (Isaiah 40:3-5).

Thus a shalom spirituality is fundamentally a missionary spirituality, a recognition that the kingdoms of this world, with all their living death and dying life, are not our home. We do not live in two kingdoms, Martin Luther notwithstanding.

THE LION OF JUDAH AND LION-TAMERS

Jesus spent his ministry proclaiming the kingdom of God while defeating the kingdom of Satan. He defeated it once and for all. We live in an already/not yet world where God has come and is coming; where we are simultaneous saints and sinners, forgiven and damned; where prophecy is fulfilled and promised; where the best is to be hoped for and the worst is to be expected; where the forces of destruction, having been defeated, are victorious in disintegration; where everything is different and nothing is different. We are conscripts of a strange new age, claimed by a future touched and transformed by the past.

If a shalom spirituality is based on a covenant of peace where, in Brueggeman's words, "all of creation is one, every creature in community with every other, living in harmony and security toward the joy and well-being of every other creature,"[17] then peacemakers will have entered into the reality of a new way of living, into a kingdom that is not a place but a people, into a church that demonstrates both the fruit-bearing of the faithful and the first fruits of the future. As a paradigm of what is emerging, a Christbody community of peacemakers will live harmoniously on all fronts: economical, ecological, ecclesiastical.

A shalom spirituality will have revolutionary consequences for the economic and social dimensions of peace. Second Kings 7:3-9 is a parable of American history. The four lepers who escaped the siege of Samaria represent the outcast and marginal people who settled the New World. The settlers found in their Aramean camp (the American wilderness) wealth and resources that were not theirs. They initially took what belonged to others and began hoarding. We continue to replicate that initial pattern. While the world out there was starving, we amassed enough for everyone. Every now and then our consciences tingle: "What we are doing is not right. This is a day of good news and we are keeping it to ourselves" (verse 9). We realize we have what it takes to release a world under siege. But we can still be found "keeping it to ourselves," as our besieged brothers and sisters become angrier and angrier.

It is estimated that every adult American loses at least $100 in cash each year. This is as much money as millions of families in underdeveloped countries make in a year. It is partly our greed that contributes to such behavior as found in the ghetto of Washington, D.C., where "getting paid" is slang for mugging somebody. In the shalom community, "getting paid" will be everyone's due for working in a society of fruitful fields and freedom from famine, a society structured so that peace and prosperity, love and justice are not divisible. In a shalom spirituality, there is sharing instead of greed, forgiveness instead of vengeance, and restitution instead of the amnesty of amnesia. In a shalom community, the scales of justice have been adjusted so that the meek inherit the earth.

A shalom spirituality is based on a right relationship between creatures and creation. As it is now, humanity resembles what more than one scholar is calling a "planetary cancer" on the surface of the earth, a malignant growth of egocentric cells eating away and reproducing themselves indiscriminately, all the while cannibalizing their host body. We live in a world of such tumorous rapaciousness that the worst thing one can do to a plant or an animal is place it on an endangered species list. It just makes them more desirable to collectors, whose juices are stimulated by such adventures as digging up Venus's-flytraps from marshes or killing rhinos to rip out their unicornish horns. The species *Homo sapiens* is responsible for almost as many if not more extinctions than the series of disasters that destroyed the dinosaurs. In a shalom spirituality, love of nature does not take a backseat to love of neighbor. Peacemakers live nonviolently with their environment.

Finally, a shalom spirituality builds an ecclesiastical household where the human spirit can find both roof and hearth, as Hilaire Belloc would express it. In other words, a shalom community has solved two of the greatest mysteries of the universe: who are the members of the Lion's pride, and how should those members live with one another. We are the Lion's pride when we live together as a messianic community—a community joining former enemies under one roof—and as a eucharistic community—a community where hearth-and-table fellowship is as decisive as it was for Jesus (Matthew 8:11; 22:1-14) and Jeremiah: "Did not your fathers eat and drink and do justice and righteousness? Then it was well with him. He judged the cause of the poor and needy; then it was well. Is this not to know me? says the Lord" (22:15-16 RSV).

It used to be said that if Jesus came to a Methodist church without a covered dish, he probably wouldn't be let in. Few things nicer could be said about Methodists. For if shedding each other's blood makes us enemies, eating each other's food makes us friends. The eucharistic meal celebrates our new identity as a body of Christ, an organism where the people we hate, and who hate us, are bound to us. We cannot pray any farther than the first two words of the Disciples' Prayer ("Our Father") without praying for our enemies and making our enemies our friends. For if a Jew excludes a Gentile from the word "Our," or an Arab a Jew, or a Brahmin a pariah, or a South African an Afrikaner, then he or she is excluding him- or herself from the word "Father," from the God who is *Abba-Imma* to us all.

When people say they're looking for a friendly church, what they really mean is that they are looking for a church of friends. I once visited a church where the couple sitting next to the aisle passed me the "Ritual of Friendship" pad. After I had filled it out, they returned it to the pew-rack without ever looking at it. As difficult as friendship with the stranger may be, it is often an easier thing than friendship with family and friends.[18] James Breech argues in *The Silence of Jesus* that it is the person sitting at the table, not the person lying by the roadside, who presents the real trial to love.

Many people would be willing to sacrifice their lives, if necessary, out of "love" for another. But such acts of immediate heroism which occur as it were on a stage with everyone watching, and which terminate the ordeal of living in the presence of the concrete other, are not to be confused with love of neighbour, which means hard work and tenacity, and which involves learning to affirm the actual other who sits across from one at the table, whether his or her table manners are graceful or ungraceful, his or her conversation engaging or boring, his or her habits mannerly or ill-mannered. The prayer that Jesus taught his table companions to say before sitting down to eat and drink together shows that Jesus understood the fundamental dynamics of such occasions, that it was during that time, as perhaps at no other, that they were most in need of that power which would sustain them in their readiness to be present in fellowship.[19]

Martin Buber declared that our highest human duty is to transform society into community.[20] But Jesus did not say for us to bring the kingdom in. Jesus said for us to receive the kingdom as a gift (Mark 4:26-29). We say, "Thine is the kingdom, and the power, and the glory." But we think, "Yes, Lord, it's your kingdom, but it comes by *our* power, so give us part of the glory." A shalom spirituality is not found in the arrogant delusion that we can build the kingdom of God on earth, which even Jesus did not do. There never has been a "just society"—a faith that is contingent on justice denies the historical record and dumps our ancestors' experiences of God. A shalom spirituality is not found by living in justice, but by living in faith. "The just shall live by faith." A shalom spirituality is not the peacemakers' way of showing the world how much they can build real kingdom koinonia. Rather, as Parker Palmer insists, a shalom community is God's way of showing the world that only God can build a kingdom koinonia.

Like the shell on a snail's back, a shalom community is both our home and our handicap, both a protection and a burden. Peacemakers are the body of Christ in spite of, not because of themselves.

CHAPTER 6

A Race of Hawks, Owls, and Doves

> I have seen pictures of huge, ungainly prehistoric monsters who developed such a weight of protective shell that they sank under its burden and became extinct. Our civilization likewise is sinking under the burden of nuclear defense, and may well soon be extinct.
>
> —Malcolm Muggeridge, *Things Past*

The dove, the hawk, and the owl have come to symbolize the three basic stances on war and peace in western civilizations: no-war (dove), pro-war (hawk), and just-war (owl). Historically, the Christian tradition has accepted the morality of two kinds of warfare: the holy war and the just war. The holy war tradition, so prominent in the early life of Israel, is misinterpreted as an unremitting call to warfare rather than an unremitting call to holiness. The tooth-and-claw strategy is as much a caricature of Old Testament attitudes towards violence as the turned-cheek strategy is of New Testament patterns of confronting evil. More often than not, the violence in the history of Israel fits into the "plans, but not of my devising, . . . schemes, but not inspired by me" category mentioned by Isaiah (30:1).

Studies by Peter C. Craigie and Millard C. Lind have demonstrated that Jesus creatively reworked his Old Testament heritage rather than introducing a new perspective; that the "Crucified God" is an unfolding, not an overturning, of the "Warrior God"; and that the Hebrew tradition accented the power and might of God, not of military heroes and machines.[1] When Samuel was unduly impressed by the appearance of Jesse's eldest son Eliab, Yahweh said: "Do not consider his appearance or his height. . . . Man looks at the outward appearance, but the Lord looks at the heart" (I Samuel 16:7 NIV).

The refusal of Israelites to celebrate war as Yahweh's instrument for accomplishing the divine way in the world is evident throughout Hebrew history. Even to the time of David, Israel rejected competing with its Philistine and Canaanite enemies in the military development and deployment of sophisticated weapons of warfare such as chariots and horses. The absence of monuments or festivals marking Israel's military victories speaks volumes about the Hebrews' ultimate reliance not on military warfare and weaponry but on God. The final thrust of the Old Testament's theology of warfare contradicts at every turn the current formulations of holy-war/pro-war doctrines. The Old Testament position is best expressed in Zechariah 4:6 (RSV): "Not by might, nor by power, but by my Spirit, says the Lord of hosts." The worldwide resurgence of religious violence shows that the holy-war tradition is still very much alive in Judaism (e.g., the Jewish Defense League), Islam (e.g., extremist Shiite Moslems), and Christianity (e.g., the Protestant-Catholic conflict in Ulster). But the hawk is as yet not a serious threat to the owls and doves in the race to win the human heart.

Pacifism is so rooted in the soil of Christian tradition that no-war doctrines stand as one of the most distinctive contributions of Christianity to the world of political and moral theory. In fact, Peter Brock argues that up until the nineteenth century pacifism in the West was limited to Christians.[2] All varieties of pacifism are based on the conviction that the end does not justify the means, that a methodology cannot be adopted which is inconsistent with an eschatology. The famous Suarez formula is wrong: "If the end is lawful, the necessary means are also lawful." A technique of violence cannot be justified even by a teleology of peace. Just because our enemy is doing it does not justify our doing it. For pacifists, "backfire bombers" are well named, for bombings always backfire. Violence breeds violence, never peace.

Sir Thomas More's image of controversialists as "very much like to men fighting naked among piles of stones: each has plenty of weapons, neither has any defense"[3] conveys sharply the pacifist frustration over the ineradicable stupidity and futility of using military instruments to achieve moral ideals. For Christian pacifists the methods are as simple as laboring the point once again: The gospel requires us to feed the hungry, clothe the naked, visit the prisoner, and welcome the homeless. War requires us to do just the opposite.

All is not right with most forms of pacifist doctrines, however. For one thing, the issue among pacifists has often been less one of eschatology than one of escapology: an escape from ambiguous predicaments where relative values reign supreme; an evading of responsibility for making less than ideal choices; an evacuation from a wanton, war-torn world where being a Christian and a citizen conflict; and a denial of the wrong we all do in our struggle to do right. A telling objection against milksop pacifism has always been the charge that pacifists place a higher premium on guarding their own consciences, keeping their own hands clean, and preserving their own purity, than on saving neighbors' lives. The burden of proof is on pacifists to demonstrate how what they are doing is different from nothing.

Second, pacifists all too easily scramble moral categories between individuals and states. Even the non-pacifist Reinhold Niebuhr admitted Jesus was a pacifist. The question, however, is not whether war is the way of love, or what did Jesus do, but what are we to do when states cannot live according to the Beatitudes? The issue here is not the desultory, delusory applicability of morality to social and governmental structures. The three simple words "Jesus is Lord" rearrange relationships among states as well as peoples. The issue is one of pluralism: singing the Lord's song in a foreign land. The issue is one of acculturation: singing a foreign song in the Lord's land.

Third, from a historian's viewpoint, a pacifist between wars is like a prohibitionist between drinks (as Episcopal bishop Paul Jones first argued in the 1920s). It is one thing to be a pacifist when one is safe, or even when others are being attacked. It is another thing to be a pacifist when you are expected obediently to put your head in the gas oven, or when bombs are falling in your own backyard. Pacifist conviction has often been like a shimmering cobweb, its fragile beauty easily smashed by the first drops of rain.

Finally, pacifists in the twentieth century, from the Quakers to Gandhi, have built their belief, blasts of reality notwithstanding, around a noble faith in the basic goodness and reasonableness of human nature, naively winking at sin, waving as it passes by, or waiving its penalties. Failure to acknowledge that while God may work in mysterious ways, so can the devil, is the religious equivalent of the famous issue of the *London Daily Express* of August 7, 1939, when ten out of twelve of its European correspondents reported blissfully that "there will be no war this year." Hitler is the single best argument against pacifism.

Just-war theories rival pacifism as the most powerful and authentic Christian responses to evil in the history of the church. The just-war tradition says that no war is ever really honorable or holy. But in cases where the question is not what wins the most but what fails the least, war can be unavoidable and right. In those instances, although war cannot be fought decently, at least it can be fought justly and in close keeping with classical moral tradition. As Martin Luther states so clearly in *Whether Soldiers, Too, Can Be Saved* (1527), war can be a form of police action to preserve freedom, justice, and peace. Just as the state is responsible for policing and punishing the citizenry to maintain law and order, so by extension the state has the right to use the violence of war to punish evil, protect the good, and preserve peace. In international law, the principles of a just war are most fully expressed in the Hague and Geneva Conventions and the First Additional Protocol. In short, the just-war tradition repudiates the notion that "all is fair in love and war."

All is not right, however, with just-war theory either. For starters, it has never worked. As we have seen (chapter 4), the Christian faith has not significantly restrained America's involvement in war or effectively limited the violence of international strife. Just as medieval theologians dressed up classical moral theory in Christian garb and called it "just war," so American Christians have dressed up the nation's bellicose deeds in Christian language and called it "just war." Just-war doctrines make no pretense about being derived from biblical principles. Just war is a political theory, and politics governs its logic as surely as politics have governed America's justification for its wars. Just-war rhetoric has functioned as a smokescreen for just-any-old American war.

Second, just war is predicated on the fundamental principle that there are people just enough to fight a war. As flawed as this principle is, for the sake of argument let us assume a level of moral and motivational purity that does not exist. Let us also assume not only a people just enough but a cause just enough for war, forgetting, for the moment, to question our right to be judge of what is just.

There are two primary principles of how a just war should be fought. The first is the principle of discrimination, which assures noncombatant immunity (i.e., you do not shoot the wounded, the innocent, or civilians). The second is the principle of proportionality, which states that destruction should be in strict proportion to military necessity. Both of these principles are obviously impossible to maintain in modern warfare. Nuclear/technological weaponry "defends selectively, but kills collectively."[4] When the B-29 *Bockscar* dropped its "Fat Man" bomb (named after Winston Churchill) on Nagasaki, the vast majority of those annihilated were the elderly and small children (and Catholics). Only 3 percent of the dead were members of the military. When the *Enola Gay* dropped its "Little Boy" cargo, the dead at the Hiroshima "military base" included twenty American airmen in a prisoner of war camp and six thousand Japanese children who were on their way to school when the bomb exploded.

The collected stories of *hibakusha* children graphically reveal the new look of war and the "justice" in a "just" war: a woman burned so badly you couldn't tell her back from her front; an old man with sores and burns swarming with thousands of squirming maggots; a junior high student trying to douse the fire burning his clothes with the blood gushing from his wounds; instantly white-haired high school girls literally skinned alive, nude bodies of raw flesh wrapped at the wrists and ankles by skin peeled in red strips like potato skins; children wandering aimlessly in a procession of death, tightly clutching what is left of each other's blackened hands; the fingers of one human hand swollen into giant balloons, another burning with a blue flame; a blood-drenched child standing on the street looking at the ruins of his house, shaking a pot, stomping his feet and screaming at the top of his lungs; a charred baby cradled by its dazed father as it dies searching for the breasts of its dead mother.[5]

I reproduce these awful pictures "lest you forget the things which your eyes have seen," in the words of Deuteronomy 4:9 (RSV). Will we forget what our eyes, and even our children's eyes, have seen? We can see; the bomb is blind. It cannot distinguish between infants and infantry. From the very nature of the bomb, what we mistakenly call nuclear "war" knocks out the underpinnings from the only plausible ethical foundation for a just war. A "just war" ends up being just war.

A RACE OF HAWKS, OWLS, AND DOVES

In recent years, the owlish perspective has found renewed support in areas of the world where liberation theologians have imbibed the Marxist myth that the only development strategy worth pursuing is armed revolution. Despite this, the owl has been losing ground to the dove faster than it has for at least a millennium. Indeed, one of the most salient features of contemporary Christian views on war and peace is not merely that the dove has perhaps a larger lead and following than at any time since the fourth century, or that institutional Christianity now seems to be lining up en masse behind pacifist forms of expression more than at any time since 1945. It is rather that the owl and dove are mating for the first time in history.

The owl and the dove have discovered that they have more in common than they ever imagined. Both pacifism and just-war doctrines are gifts to the world from the Christian religion. Both pacifists and just-warriors theoretically limit the sanction of and participation in violence, whether the law-and-order violence of the right or the liberation violence of the left. Both recognize a vast range of violent actions, from spanking, unnecessary surgery, and sports, to fistfights, bombing sorties, and full-scale invasions. Both impose limits beyond which one must, at considerable sacrifice, say no! to one sort of violence or another. Both recognize a spot on the spectrum of resistance when one should be willing to die rather than use violence. Both castigate the rationalizations under which nearly all wars have been fought. Both take the romance out of war, and face the horrors of war in their full ghastliness. Both act out of love and reconciliation; both are courting each other, and need each other, like never before, because of their common cause of opposition to nuclear weapons. The genius of *In Defense of Creation* is the bishops' desire to rise above the old pacifist/non-pacifist argument to lay before America the transcendency of peacemaking for all of us. Indeed, peacemaking today requires that owls and doves learn to sit on the same limb.

In the Garden of Gethsemane (John 18:7-11) Jesus offered a pattern for owls and doves to follow which enables them to transcend their differences in the cause of peace. We can unite behind Jesus in economies of will, economies of forgiveness, and economies of love.

First, *economies of will.* Jesus did not run from those who disagreed with him, or even from those who plotted his death. Jesus' way of dealing with violence was to step out into a face-to-face meeting with his opponents, thereby acknowledging that enemies too are brothers and sisters, worth getting to know, worth listening to, worth caring for and even dying for. Dale Aukerman calls this "The Scandal of Defenselessness" in his modern classic on peace, *The Darkening Valley:* "Reconciliation could be brought about only if he drew near to the enemy, met them, spoke with them, showed Himself to them. It could come only through defenselessness, vulnerability, the cross."[6] Jesus did not only die for his friends and family. Jesus willfully died for his enemies. Jesus identified himself with both the victims of injustice and the unjust oppressors. Jesus went to the cross, a lamb to the slaughter, out of love for the butcher. Jesus died that butchers like Hitler and Khomeni might live and be loved. Would that Christians who disagree over ways to peace would show even a smidgin of such charity to each other, not to speak of to their enemies. Christians willfully pitch their tents behind enemy lines.

But there are other angles to these economies of will than the courage of redemptive confrontation. A steel will untempered by a supple spirit of goodwill to those who disagree with us violates Jesus' pattern. One of the sentences I remember most in Martin E. Marty's Himalayan height of writings is this: "There is no such thing as Christian action, only Christian motivation." In other words, there is not one "peace plan," or even one morally pure peace policy. We must be careful not to give official Christian status to either dovish or owlish programs for peace and denounce other people as kneeling at altars of alien faiths. Jesus lavished on the faith of a soldier the loftiest praise of his ministry (Matthew 8:10). We come to peace on different roads, depending on our time in history and our life experiences.

It simply will not do for unconditional pacifists to tell black Christian South Africans who have seen their children gunned down by police—a ten-year-old unarmed boy shot in Soweto out of "self-defense" (the boy's hysterical mother restrained from running to him by a police officer who sneered, "Let the bastard die"); a six-year-old girl walking up the steps to her home shot in the back by the police out of "mistaken identity" ("We thought it was a dog")—that there is a politically effective, nonviolent answer to the problem of oppression and aggression. It simply will not wash to tell Christian politicians, police, and military personnel, who have to deal on a daily basis with the moral decay of the world and with restraining wickedness though institutions which enforce order and preserve and protect human life, that like Phinehas of Numbers 25, who killed the person who broke the covenant and thereby brought down God's wrath, they should not be celebrated as heroes of peacemaking. It simply will not do to tell scientists who live every day with the responsibility for the nightmare of nuclear weapons being built and controlled by sinful, untrustworthy human beings at best (and by terrorists, hijackers, and kidnappers at worst), that unilateral disarmament is the only Christian path to peace. It simply will not work to tell a Daughters of the American Revolution convention that unconditional pacifism is the only authentic stance that Christians should have ever adopted, or to tell the NAACP that anytime evil is overcome with violence, as in the slave uprisings, that the wrong thing was done (because after all, the New Testament did not counsel slaves to revolt but to imitate the way of the cross).

For those like United Methodist Helge Heen, a Norwegian who grew up with the Hitlers, Stalins, and other well-armed bandits of World War II, peacemakers allow for the possibility that some Christians may have a basis for arguing that violence may need to be used for peace's sake. The following is an excerpt from his personal response to the Council of Bishops' *In Defense of Creation:*

I am for peace, always have been and always will be. This letter is about PEACE.

I grew up in the country of Norway. In my youth I was full of idealistic thoughts and plans. I was convinced that if there were no armies there would be no war. Therefore we should abandon all military in all countries.

In 1940, Norway had a very weak military because the Norwegians generally believed there was nothing anybody could want in Norway and besides, if you had a weak military, you would not be a threat to anyone and therefore no one would bother to attack us.

The following consequences were the result of this reasoning:
1. Hitler's Germany attacked Norway in April 1940 and within a month had conquered the whole country.
2. Relatively few died in this conflict. The dead could be counted in the thousands.
3. The following occupation which lasted for five years was dreadful. The dead during the occupation could be counted in the tens of thousands. Many were sent to concentration camps and/or tortured. Many died there and most of those few who made it back were maimed for life both mentally and physically. Others were shot or killed directly.

Ever since that time, the Norwegian Government has placed much more emphasis on defense and the military. They will not make the same mistake ever again.

I was still young and did not listen to all this. My conviction was strong. After High School I entered the compulsory service in the Norwegian Army and served my term but always with a negative attitude toward defense.

Later, I went to college in Switzerland. There I learned that Hitler did not attack Switzerland because they had an excellent defense. An attack would have been too costly and would not have succeeded in conquering all of Switzerland. The Swiss can produce a fighting army of 500,000 soldiers in twenty-four hours. As a matter of fact, they have an old democracy dating back to the 13th century. In order to survive, they have always maintained a strong defense and been ready to defend themselves when the need has arisen. The Swiss are a free, peaceloving, democratic people. It was in Switzerland that I finally came to the conclusion that a strong defense means peace and a weak defense invited war and occupation. The latter may lead to repression, concentration camps, torture and mass killings. The examples of Norway and Switzerland are very clear.

There are many recent examples of wars. These have all started because of poor defense in the country being invaded. Such examples are:
  1. The Falkland Islands.
    There were less than one hundred soldiers on the Falkland Islands when Argentina attacked.
  2. Iran.
    Iran had just had a revolution. The military had been decimated. Most of the military equipment was not operating and spare parts were not readily available when Iraq attacked.
  3. Afganistan.
    There was disarray in Afganistan when Russia moved their troops into that country and with a standing army of 70 to 80,000 soldiers this was a pushover for Russia. Especially so since most of the troops sided with the Russians.

The lessons from these wars are all the same: The war started because the attacker thought the conquering of the country in question would be a pushover. In history, I have never seen a case where the attacker thought he was going to lose. The attacker is always looking for a victory. This does not always mean the attacker wins; but that is because he made errors in judgment.

The final conclusion is that peace can only be secured by a strong defense and those who honestly are seeking peace must support a strong defense.[7]

We advocate one "peace plan" over another, trusting not in our own morally superior position but in God's forgiving grace. We should not expect all Christians to have the same theology of peace. We should expect all Christians, however, to be motivated by a common will for peace. We differ over means, and can fight about that difference vigorously because we acknowledge each other as siblings in Christ and worship together as part of the same family. For this reason economies of will do not play politics with the body of Christ. They put controversy and debate back into the body without tearing the body apart.

Second, *economies of forgiveness*. Jesus told Peter, "Put your sword into its sheath; shall I not drink the cup which the Father has given me?" (John 18:11 RSV). In the garden, Jesus lived out the nonresistance that he preached on the Mount (Matthew 5:38-42). To quote Dale Aukerman once again: "God did not defend himself. The Father did not defend the Son."[8] Or in the words of I Peter 2:23 (RSV), "When he was reviled, he did not revile in return; when he suffered, he did not threaten." Economies of forgiveness rule out all thought of self-defense or retaliation.

When somebody butts in line, we stick up for our rights. Economies of forgiveness teach us that we butt in lines all the time ourselves (our economic policies and relationship with nature are but two obvious examples). If we expect God to display mercy toward us, we had better display mercy toward other line-butters. We all live lives of "forgiven violence" where "no act is without sin and no policy without need of forgiveness."[9]

We are all inextricably entangled in the web of violence. To do violence is to rape the humanity or integrity of a person, whether through institutional, quiet, or indirect forms of violence, which some call "structural violence" but is better called "social injustice," or through the legal or illegal use of force to harm someone physically. It is not only the ten million Americans who earn their livelihood preparing for nuclear war, or the one-third of the world's scientists and engineers who are directly or indirectly working on military matters, who are part of the demonic arms race. We are all guilty of moral involvement in violence. We are all confederates in the conspiracy of war. Complicity with violence is locked into our lives, and our everyday jobs, weekly paychecks, and monthly bills are part of a programme of nuclearism and violence. The place for Christians to be is not on some nonexistent plane of purity. Living out of grace in the midst of violence must be our stance in the world. This means an active dialectic of forgiveness: toward the attacker or intruder, toward the one who responds to the attack or intrusion.

Economies of forgiveness also rule out personal retaliation or self-defense, because Jesus calls us to be peacemakers in our personal relationships, "leaving you an example, that you should follow in his steps" (I Peter 2:21 RSV). Recent writers have even begun to develop economies of forgiveness which regulate our response to evil. Peter Hinchliff calls this a "politics of forgiveness."[10] It acknowledges the enormity of evil, the inevitability of guilt, and the ineradicable promise of a new future creatively reshaped out of human fraility and sin. Jonathan Schell has begun to build a policy of "pre-emptive repentance" on Jesus' teachings of forgiveness, in which a form of "moral deterrence" takes over from "strategic deterrence." "We must repent the crime before we commit it," Schell argues, "and in that repentance find the will not to commit it."[11]

Finally, economies of forgiveness require us to turn the other cheek—partly because sometimes we deserve a punch in the nose. Both Jeremiah and Isaiah had to tell Israel not to defend themselves against the enemy, because they didn't deserve defense, they deserved punishment (Jeremiah 5:12-17). Like Israel, we may need to discover that a punch in the mouth really hurts.

Third, *economies of love.* In Jesus' statement to the soldiers, "I told you that I am he; so if you seek me, let these men go"

(John 18:8 RSV), there is the model of suffering love that creates economies of love. Jesus dealt with injustice by sacrificing his own life, by spilling his own blood, not the blood of his defenders and/or attackers. Jesus suffered to save others. He took upon himself the suffering of others.

The biblical ethic of love goes beyond nonviolence. Christians are not simply called to do no injury to another, or to not get involved in patterns of violence. Christians are called to seek the good of others and to promote their wholeness. Life is not every man for himself or every woman for herself. Life is rather himself for everyone, herself for everyone. This is why the ubiquitous question, What would you do if a violent attacker broke into your home? won't go away. It is one thing to answer that question when evil is being inflicted against oneself alone. It is much more complicated when nonresistance to evil means acquiescence in injustice against neighbor. Gandhi believed that to do nothing in the face of evil is worse than the use of military force. Both incur guilt, but a misdemeanor of commission incurs less guilt than a felony of omission. Violence cannot be avoided at all costs. There are some values, some principles, that may be worth more than life itself. Life is not our most precious possession. Peacemakers agree that there are things in life that we should be willing to die for, that we may have to get violent about.

Dorothy Day liked to quote Dostoevski: "Love in action is a harsh and dreadful thing compared to love in dreams." Love is not always candles and romance. To love is sometimes to bear a cross and die. Jesus died so we may live; that is the essence of the doctrine of salvation. Biological survival was sacrificed for the sake of spiritual values. The cross is a symbol that there are more important things in life than mere self-preservation. It is also a reminder that nonviolent action is not without violence. Suffering and death greet their opposition. Jesus said that there is no greater love than that a person lays down life for a friend (John 15:13). Truth, righteousness, love, justice, freedom, friendship—these are worth living for and, in some cases, worth dying for. Just as Jesus "died to make men holy," so there may be times when we must "die to make men free." The morning after the failure of the German resistance to assassinate Hitler on July 20, 1944, Henning von Tresckow spoke these parting words before taking his inevitable execution into his own hands and letting the Russians shoot him:

> God once promised to spare Sodom should there be found ten just men in the city. He will, I trust, spare Germany because of what we have done and not destroy her. None of us can complain of his lot. Whoever joined the resistance put on the shirt of Nessus. The worth of a man is certain only if he is prepared to sacrifice his life for his convictions.[12]

Survival is not an ultimate virtue for a tradition that lives the paradox that to lose one's life is to gain it. The gospel replaces the instinct for survival with the impetus for sacrificial love.

The Christian lives by the norm of nonviolence, but allows for (never approves of) the exception. There are occasions when Christians may find the use of force inevitable in loving our neighbors and to fighting the evils of society. Even though Jesus taught us not how to kill but how to die, peacemakers must allow for the occurrence, on the jagged edges of existence, of some dreadful instances when taking someone's life to protect other lives is part of an economy of love.

There may be situations where some Christians prayerfully determine that only shedding blood can prevent further bloodletting. Leo Tolstoy's famous essay against violence, "Certain Things Christians Cannot Do," fails to consider the fact that as soon as one names those absolute obligations one can think of situations where those "things" are precisely what Christians morally have to do.[13] For example, it is possible to invent a scenario where a national Christian leader could be forced to choose between two evils: genocide or guerilla warfare. All doves and some owls will trust God to work through genocide. Some owls will trust God to work through war. But both are still Christians, for both are servants of shalom.

The Christian's passion is peacemaking. In fact, owls and doves can perch on the same limb because both owls and doves share a peacemaker's heartbeat. Peacemaking is not the same thing as principled opposition to all forms of violence, the reigning philosophy of pacifism prevalent in America today. An owl is a peacemaker who supports the use of physical force "at the very last hour and in the darkest of days," as Karl Barth puts it.[14] In fact, all Christians can even be defined as pacifists (but not all pacifists can be defined as Christians) in the original meaning of the word. The first time the word "pacifism" is known to have occurred was in 1902 when a Frenchman, attending an international peace congress, announced that by "pacifism" he meant "anti-warism."[15] The true pacifist spirit is perhaps most pungently expressed in the Walt Whitman quotation Harry Emerson Fosdick was so fond of loudly proclaiming throughout Riverside Church: "I say God damn the wars—all wars: God damn every war: God damn 'em! God damn 'em!"

Christians are people who see war as damnably and intrinsically evil. The general who gutted Georgia, William Tecumseh Sherman, addressed a convention of Civil War veterans in 1880 with these words: "There is many a boy here today who looks on war as all glory, but boys, it is all hell." "War is hell," as we have shortened Sherman's pithy statement, and there cannot possibly be anything worse than hell. War is never "justified" or "sacred" for the same reason a cancer is never "justified" or "sacred." God may work through cancers or war, and sometimes we may be forced to go through hell, but God's wrenching good from evil does not legitimate or sanctify either cancers or war.

Christians will want to say more than this. But they will not say less.

CHAPTER 7

A Postscript Parable

He sent out His messengers preaching this peace, His apostles who spread this grace abroad through the whole world, who shone as bright, burning torches before all men, so that they might lead me and all erring sinners into the right way. . . . Their words I love, their practices I follow.
—Meno Simons, "Meditations on the Twenty-Fifth Psalm"

Wishing to encourage her young son's progress on the piano, a mother took her boy to a Paderewski concert. After they were seated, the mother spotted a friend in the audience and walked down the aisle to greet her. Seizing the opportunity to explore the wonders of the concert hall, the little boy rose and eventually explored his way through a door marked "NO ADMITTANCE." When the houselights dimmed and the concert was about to begin, the mother returned to her seat and discovered that the child was missing. Suddenly, the curtains parted and spotlights focused on the impressive Steinway on stage.

In horror, the mother saw her little boy sitting at the keyboard, innocently picking out "Twinkle, Twinkle Little Star." At that moment, the great piano master made his entrance, quickly moved to the piano, and whispered in the boy's ear, "Don't quit. Keep playing." Then leaning over, Paderewski reached down with his left hand and began filling in a bass part. Soon his right arm reached around to the other side of the child and he added a running obligato. Together, the old master and the young novice transformed a frightening situation into a wonderfully creative experience. And the audience was mesmerized.

Whatever our situation in life and history—however outrageous, however desperate, whatever dry spell of the spirit, whatever dark night of the soul—God is whispering deep within our beings, "Don't quit. Keep playing. You are not alone. Together we will transform the broken patterns into a masterwork of my creative art. Together, we will mesmerize the world with our song of peace."

Notes

Introduction

1. Chana Bloch, *Spelling the Word: George Herbert and the Bible* (Berkeley: University of California, 1985), 29.
2. G. K. Chesterton, *St. Francis of Assisi* (New York: George H. Doran, 1924), 102-3.
3. Richard T. McSorley, *Peace Eyes* (Washington, D.C.: Center for Peace Studies, Georgetown University, 1978).
4. Yasuo C. Furuya, "The Baptism of the Atomic Bomb," *The Christian Century* (July 30–August 6, 1980): 760.

1. Not All Geese Are Swans

1. E. P. Thompson, "Notes on Exterminism, the Last Stage of Civilization," in *Exterminism and Cold War,* ed. *New Left Review* (London: New Left Review, 1982), 5.
2. United Methodist Church (U.S.), Council of Bishops, *In Defense of Creation: The Nuclear Crisis and a Just Peace* (Nashville: Graded Press, 1986); Christian Church (Disciples of Christ), Panel on Christian Ethics in a Nuclear Age, *Seeking God's Peace in a Nuclear Age: A Call to Disciples of Christ* (St. Louis: C.B.P. Press, 1985); Lutheran Church in America, Division for Mission in North America, *Peace and Politics* (New York: Division for Mission in North America, Lutheran Church in America, 1984); Catholic Church, National Conference of Catholic Bishops, *The Challenge of Peace: God's Promise and Our Response: A Pastoral Letter on War and Peace* (Washington, D.C.: United States Catholic Conference, 1983); American Lutheran Church, *Mandate for Peacemaking: A Statement of*

the American Lutheran Church (Minneapolis: Augsburg, 1982); Episcopal Church, Joint Commission on Peace, *To Make Peace* (Cincinnati: Forward Movement Publications, 1982); Paul Abrecht and Ninan Kosby, eds., *Before It's Too Late: The Challenge of Nuclear Disarmament* (Geneva: World Council of Churches, 1983); Reformed Church in America, General Synod, 1981, "Christian Imperatives for Peacemaking," in *Acts and Proceedings of the General Synod* 61 (1981): 66-69; United Presbyterian Church in the U.S.A., 192nd General Assembly, *Peacemaking: The Believer's Calling* (New York: The Assembly, 1980); Norvel Hadley, ed., *New Call to Peacemaking: A Challenge to All Friends* (Philadelphia: The Faith and Life Movement, 1976). See also *To Proclaim Peace: Religious Communities Speak Out on the Arms Race,* comp. and ed. John Donaghy for the Fellowship of Reconciliation, 2nd rev. ed. (Nyack, N.Y.: Fellowship Publications, 1983); and "Appendix IV," in Arthur C. Cochrane, *The Mystery of Peace* (Elgin, Ill.: Brethren Press, 1986), 177-78.

3. David Riesman, "The Overriding Issue," *Commonweal* 107 (May 23, 1980): 299-301.

4. Lutheran Peace Fellowship (American Lutheran Church), *Peace Notes* 1, no. 1 (November 1983).

5. Ralph E. Lapp, "The Einstein Letter That Started It All," *New York Times Magazine* (August 2, 1964): 54; Ronald W. Clark, *Einstein: The Life and Times* (New York: World Publishing Co., 1971), 591.

6. For the ways in which the current discussion about nuclear weapons revolves around recycled questions and arguments from the period 1945 to 1950, see Paul S. Boyer, *By the Bomb's Early Light: American Thought and Culture at the Dawn of the Atomic Age* (New York: Pantheon, 1987).

7. The Public Agenda Foundation, *Voter Options on Nuclear Arms Policy: A Briefing Book for the 1984 Elections* (New York: Public Agenda Foundation, 1984).

8. Jerome D. Frank, *Sanity and Survival: Psychological Aspects of War and Peace* (New York: Random House, 1967), 34.

9. James Turner Johnson, *Can Modern War Be Just?* (New Haven: Yale University Press, 1984), 85.

10. Jeremy Taylor, *The Rule and Exercises of Holy Living Containing the Whole Duty of a Christian,* reprinted in *The Practical Works of Jeremy Taylor,* vol. 2 (London: Henry G. Bohn, 1850), 8.

11. Karl Barth, *Church Dogmatics,* vol. 3, part 4 (Edinburgh: T. & T. Clark, 1961), 453.

12. Stephen Spender, "Ultima Ratio Regum," in his *Collected Poems, 1928–1985* (New York: Random House, 1986), 69.

13. Jonathan Schell, *The Fate of the Earth* (New York: Alfred A. Knopf, 1982).

14. For the comparison of the threatened annihilation of multitudes of civilians by nuclear weapons to genocide, see Leo Kuper, *The Prevention of Genocide* (New Haven: Yale University Press, 1986).

15. Quoted by Harold Freeman, *If You Give a Damn About Life* (New York: Dodd Mead, 1985), 28.

16. Helmut Thielicke, *Theological Ethics,* vol. 2 (Philadelphia: Fortress Press, 1969), 419.

17. Elaine Scarry, *The Body in Pain: The Making and Unmaking of the World* (New York: Oxford University Press, 1985).

18. Robert Scheer, *With Enough Shovels: Reagan, Bush, and Nuclear War* (New York: Random House, 1982), 18, 22.

19. For the special investment of women in peace research and the unique contributions feminist studies are making to peace values, see Birgit Brock-Utne, *Educating for Peace: A Feminist Perspective* (New York: Pergamon Press, 1985); Barbara Roberts, "The Death of Machothink: Feminist Research and the Transfiguration of Peace Studies," *Women's Studies International Forum* 7 (1984): 195-200; Betty Reardon, *Sexism and the War System* (New York: Teachers College Press, 1985); Leila J. Rupp, "War Is Not Healthy for Children and Other Living Things: Reflections on the Impact of Total War on Women," in *The Home Front and War in the 20th Century* (Colorado Springs: United States Air Force Academy, 1982), 156-75.

20. Dylan Thomas, "A Refusal to Mourn the Death by Fire, of a Child in London," in *The Poems of Dylan Thomas,* ed. Daniel Jones, (New York: New Directions, 1971), 196-97.

21. Adam Roberts, "The Relevance of Laws of War in the Nuclear Age," in *Nuclear Weapons, the Peace Movement and the Law,* ed. John Dewars et al. (London: Macmillan, 1986), 31.

22. Peter Porter, *Preaching to the Converted* (London: Oxford University Press, 1972), 13-14.

23. E. P. Thompson, "A Letter to America," in *Protest and Survive,* ed. E. P. Thompson and Dan Smith (New York: Monthly Review Press, 1981), 52.

24. Albert Einstein, "Atomic War or Peace," in *Out of My Later Years* (New York: Philosophical Library, 1950), 199.

25. Richard J. Mouw, "Being with the Lamb: A Sermon," *Sojourners* 10 (March 1981): 22.

26. W. H. Auden, "September 1, 1939," in *The English Auden: Poems, Essays, and Dramatic Writings, 1927–1939,* ed. Edward Mendelson (New York: Random House, 1977), 246.

27. See *To Establish the United States Academy of Peace,* report of the

Commission on Proposals for the National Academy of Peace and Conflict Resolution to the President of the United States and the Senate and House of Representatives of the United States Congress (Washington, D.C.: U.S. Government Printing Office, 1981).

28. The earliest thinker about nuclearism and the first nuclear strategist was Bernard Brodie. Within six months of the bombing of Hiroshima he published a book along with the "Yale Group" in which he stated in three sentences the fundamental principle of deterrence, long since lost in a miasma of obfuscation: "Thus far the chief purpose of our military establishment has been to win wars. From now on its chief purpose must be to avert them. It can have almost no other useful purpose." Frederick S. Dunn et al., *The Absolute Weapon: Atomic Power and World Order,* ed. Bernard Brodie (New York: Harcourt Brace, 1946), 76.

2. The Hunter and the Shepherd

1. Robert Moats Miller, *Harry Emerson Fosdick: Preacher, Pastor, Prophet* (New York: Oxford University Press, 1985), 92.

2. Martin Luther King, Jr., *Stride Toward Freedom: The Montgomery Story* (New York: Harper, 1958), 103.

3. Edward Westermarck, *The Origin and Development of the Moral Ideal,* vol. 1, 2nd ed. (London: Macmillan, 1912-17), 362.

4. H. A. Williams, *Some Day I'll Find You: An Autobiography* (London: Mitchell Beazley, 1982), 133.

5. Tertullian, *On Idolatry,* 19, in *The Ante-Nicene Fathers,* Translations of the Writings of the Fathers Down to A.D. 325, ed. Alexander Roberts and James Donaldson, vol. 3 (Grand Rapids: Wm. B. Eerdmans, 1973), 73.

6. Roland H. Bainton, *Christian Attitudes Toward War and Peace* (New York: Abingdon Press, 1960). See also Cecil John Cadoux, *The Early Christian Attitude to War: A Contribution to the History of Christian Ethics* (London: Headley, 1919).

7. See John Helgeland, "Christians and the Roman Army A.D. 173–337," *Church History* 43 (1974): 149-63; and John Helgeland, Robert J. Daly, and J. Patout Burns, *Christians and the Military: The Early Experience* (Philadelphia: Fortress Press, 1985); James F. Childress, "Moral Discourse About War in the Early Church," in *Peace, Politics and the People of God,* ed. Paul Peachey (Philadelphia: Fortress Press, 1986), 117-33.

8. Adolph von Harnack, *Militia Christi* (Philadelphia: Fortress Press, 1981).

9. "That a good purpose, formed in the knowledge of God, should be

altered, is impossible," as quoted in John Alfred Faulkner, *Cyprian: The Churchman* (Cincinnati: Jennings and Graham, 1906), 191.

10. Hans von Campenhausen, "Christians and Military Service in the Early Church," in *Tradition and Life in the Church: Essays and Lectures in Church History*, trans. A. V. Littledale (Philadelphia: Fortress Press, 1968), 167.

11. LeRoy Walters, "The Simple Structure of the 'Just War' Theory" in Peachey, *Peace, Politics and the People of God*, 135-48.

12. Studs Terkel, *Talking to Myself: A Memoir of My Times* (New York: Pantheon Books, 1984), 328.

13. See Dale Vree, *From Berkeley to Berlin and Back* (Nashville: Thomas Nelson, 1985).

14. See David E. Powell, *Antireligious Propaganda in the Soviet Union: A Study of Mass Persuasion* (Cambridge, Mass.: The MIT Press, 1975).

15. Quoted in Harold Freeman, *If You Give a Damn About Life* (New York: Dodd, Mead, 1985), iii.

16. David M. Raup, "Extinction and Global Habitability," *University of Chicago Record* 19, no. 1 (June 7, 1985): 28.

17. Emily Dickinson, "Will There Really be a 'Morning'?" in *The Complete Poems of Emily Dickinson*, ed. Thomas H. Johnson (Boston: Little, Brown, 1960), 49-50.

18. Priit J. Vesilind and Cotton Coulson, "Two Berlins: a Generation Apart," *National Geographic* 161 (January 1982): 10-11.

3. The Day and Way of the Wolf

1. An example of this can be found in John Shea, *An Experience Named Spirit* (Chicago: Thomas More, 1983), 250-51.

2. Quoted in *Hoyt's New Cyclopedia of Practical Quotations* (New York: Funk and Wagnalls, 1926), 221.

3. Gordon Kaufman, *Theology for a Nuclear Age* (Philadelphia: Westminster Press, 1985).

4. Georgia Harkness, "A Spiritual Pilgrimage," *The Christian Century* (March 15, 1939): 350.

5. Erik Routley, *Hymns and the Faith* (Greenwich, Conn.: Seabury Press, 1956), 250.

6. Anastacia Van Burkalow, "Defense of Battle Symbolism in Hymns," *The Hymn* 17 (April 1966): 37-41.

7. As quoted by Peggy L. Shriver, "The Paradox of Inclusiveness-That-Divides," *The Christian Century* (February 22, 1984): 197.

8. Harry Kemp, "The Conquerors," in *The Home Book of Verse, American and English*, ed. Burton Egbert Stevenson, vol. 2, 9th ed. (New York: Henry Holt, 1953), 3069.

9. Vernard Eller, *War and Peace From Genesis to Revelation* (Scottdale, Penn.: Herald Press, 1984), 104.

10. Origen, *Against Celsus* 5. 33; 8. 73; in *The Ante-Nicene Fathers, Translations of the Writings of the Fathers Down to* A.D. 325, ed. Alexander Roberts and James Donaldson, vol. 4 (Grand Rapids: Wm. B. Eerdmans, 1972), 558, 668.

11. Erik Erikson, "The Galilean Sayings and the Sense of 'I'," *Yale Review* 70 (1981): 357.

12. For Gene Sharp see *Making Europe Unconquerable: The Potential of Civilian-Based Deterrence and Defense* (Philadelphia: Taylor and Francis, 1985); *Social Power and Political Freedom* (Boston: Porter Sargent, 1980); *The Politics of Nonviolent Action* (Boston: Porter Sargent, 1973). For Howard S. Brembeck see "Civilized Defense Plan," (unpublished manuscript, 1987); *The Alternative to Nuclear War* (Goshen, Ind.: Alternative World Foundation, 1985); and *Making Nuclear War Impossible* (Goshen, Ind.: News Printing Co., 1984). For Liane Norman see "The Nonviolent Alternative: An Interview with Liane Norman," *The Center Magazine* (January/February 1987): 20-26.

13. Carl Sandburg, *Abraham Lincoln: The War Years* (New York: Charles Scribner's Sons, 1939), vol. 1: 570-71, 589-90; vol. 2: 235-37; vol. 3: 224-25, 377, 482. See also Elton Trueblood, *Abraham Lincoln: Theologian of the American Anguish* (New York: Harper & Row, 1973), 34-35.

14. Pitirim A. Sorokin, "The Powers of Creative Unselfish Love," in *New Knowledge in Human Values,* ed. Abraham Maslow (New York: Harper, 1959), 3, 10-11.

15. Rainer Maria Rilke, "What Will You Do, God, When I Die?" in *Poems from the Book of Hours,* trans. Babette Deutsch (Norfolk, Conn.: New Directions, 1941), 55.

16. John Telford, ed. *The Letters of the Rev. John Wesley,* vol. 8 (London: Epworth Press, 1931), 91.

17. Gerhard Lohfink, *Jesus and Community: The Social Dimension of Christian Faith* (Philadelphia: Fortress Press, 1984).

18. Eller, *War and Peace,* 173.

19. *The Plays of Eugene O'Neill* (New York: Random House, 1955), 280. This is one of the favorite selections of Walter J. Burghardt, who first introduced me to the play in his *Grace on Crutches: Homilies for Fellow Travelers* (New York: Paulist Press, 1986), 37.

20. Ludwig Pauli, *The Alps: Archaeology and Early History* (London: Thames and Hudson, 1984).

21. I was first disturbed by this thought after reading Philip Pare, *God Made the Devil: A Ministry of Healing* (London: Darton, Longman and Todd, 1985), 35.

22. Eller, *War and Peace,* 182-88.

23. John Howton, "The Sign of Jonah," *Scottish Journal of Theology* 15 (September 1962): 288-304. Cf. John Woodhouse, "Jesus and Jonah," *The Reformed Theological Review* 43 (May–August 1984): 33-41.

4. Stalking Wild Turkeys in Tiger Country.

1. Shailer Mathews, "Manufactured Gods," in *University of Chicago Sermons,* ed. Theodore Gerald Soares (Chicago: University of Chicago Press, 1915), 59.

2. Ron Butlin, *Ragtime in Unfamiliar Bars* (London: Secker & Warburg, 1987), 41.

3. Sherman E. Johnson, "The Apostle Paul and the Riot in Ephesus," *Lexington Theological Quarterly* 14 (October 1979): 79-88.

4. Ronald A. Wells, ed., *The Wars of America: Christian Views* (Grand Rapids: Wm. B. Eerdmans, 1981). See also Alan Kreider's excellent review of this book, entitled "Christian Views on American War," *Fides et Historia* 16 (Fall–Winter 1983): 87-93.

5. Quoted in Wells, *The Wars of America,* 146.

6. Ibid., 12.

7. See A. Costandina Titus, "A-Bombs in the Backyard: Southern Nevada Adapts to the Nuclear Age," *Nevada Historical Society Quarterly* 26 (Winter 1983): 235-54.

8. See Erich Fromm, *For the Love of Life* (New York: The Free Press, 1986), 29.

9. Quoted in Susan Thistlethwaite, ed., *A Just Peace Church* (New York: United Church Press, 1986), 72.

10. Quoted in Linus Pauling, *"Science and Peace": The Nobel Peace Prize Lecture.* (Santa Barbara: Center for the Study of Democratic Institutions, 1962), 6.

11. Fromm, *For the Love of Life,* 29.

12. Serge Moscovici, *The Age of the Crowd: A Historical Treatise on Mass Psychology,* trans. J. C. Whitehouse (New York: Cambridge University Press, 1985).

13. Freeborn Garrettson, *A Dialogue Between Do-justice and Professing-Christian Dedicated to the Respective and Collective Abolition Societies* (Wilmington, Del.: Printed by Peter Brynberg, 1812), 32.

14. The most worthless of these were "educated preachers who forcibly reminded me of lettuce growing under the shade of a peach tree, or like a gosling that had got the straddles by wading in the dew, that I turn away sick and faint." Peter Cartwright, *Autobiography of Peter Cartwright* (New York: Abingdon Press, 1956), 64.

15. Kenneth Arnold, "The Feast of St. Stephen," in "God With Us,

Meditations on Incarnation at the Feasts of St. Stephen, St. John, Holy Innocents, and the Holy Name of Our Lord Jesus Christ," delivered at the Church of St. Martin in the Fields, Chestnut Hill, Pennsylvania, December 26–31, 1986.

16. John Calvin, *The Acts of the Apostles, 14–18,* Calvin's Commentaries, vol. 7, trans. John W. Fraser (Grand Rapids, Mich.: Wm. B. Eerdmans, 1966), 165-66.

17. Ibid., 166.

18. Jörg Zink, *Turn Toward Life: The Bible and Peacemaking,* trans. Victoria Rhodin (Philadelphia: Fortress Press, 1985), 64. For the fallacy of securing peace through security, see pp. 59-70.

19. Ira Chernus, *Dr. Strangegod: Or the Symbolic Meaning of Nuclear Weapons* (Columbia: University of South Carolina Press, 1986), 47.

20. Carl Sagan, "Nuclear War and Climactic Catastrophe: Some Policy Implications," *Foreign Affairs* 62 (Winter 1983/84): 257-92.

21. John Howard Yoder, "Neither Guerrilla nor *Conquista:* The Presence of the Kingdom as Social Ethic," in *Peace, Politics and the People of God,* ed. Paul Peachey (Philadelphia: Fortress Press, 1986), 105-6, 110.

22. This is the argument of Robert Webber, "Ethics and Evangelism: Learning from the Third-Century Church," *The Christian Century* (September 24, 1986): 806-8.

5. The Lion of Judah and Lion-Tamers

1. Quoted in William Klassen, " 'A Child of Peace' (Luke 10:6) in First Century Context," *New Testament Studies* 27 (1981): 497-98.

2. Charles Grandison Finney, *Lectures on Revivals of Religion,* ed. William G. McLoughlin (Cambridge, Mass.: Harvard University Press, 1960), 115-18.

3. United Methodist Church (U.S.), Council of Bishops, *In Defense of Creation: The Nuclear Crisis and a Just Peace* (Nashville: Graded Press, 1986), 56-57.

4. Martin B. Duberman, *James Russell Lowell* (Boston: Houghton Mifflin, 1966), 274.

5. Quoted by Anthony Thwait, "Alliance to the Clyde," *Times Literary Supplement,* October 2, 1981, 1125.

6. See as an example the collection edited by Charles DeBenedetti, *Peace Heroes in Twentieth-Century America* (Bloomington, Ind.: Indiana University Press, 1986), which lifts up Jane Addams, Eugene V. Debs, Norman Thomas, Albert Einstein, A. J. Muste, Norman Cousins, Martin Luther King, Jr., and the Berrigans.

7. Stanley Hauerwas, *Should War Be Eliminated? Philosophical and Theological Investigations* (Milwaukee: Marquette University Press, 1984) and *Against the Nations: War and Survival in a Liberal Society* (Minneapolis: Winston Press, 1985), 197-98.

8. Bernard Shaw, *Saint Joan,* in *Nine Plays* (New York: Dodd Mead, 1935), 1141.

9. *New York Times,* March 17, 1983, sec. A, p. 14, col. 3.

10. Frederick Lynch, *Personal Recollections of Andrew Carnegie* (Chicago: Fleming H. Revell, 1920), pp. 156-57. See also Charles S. Macfarland, *Pioneers for Peace Through Religion* (New York: Fleming H. Revell, 1946), 22.

11. Quoted in J. Joll, review of *The Invaders,* by Eva H. Haraszti, *Times Literary Supplement,* September 30, 1983, 1064.

12. Quoted in R. Buckminster Fuller, *Utopia or Oblivion: The Prospects for Humanity* (New York: Overlook Press, 1969), 288.

13. The ordinary budget of the United Nations for 1984–1985 was $1,587,159,800. The United States paid approximately 25 percent of the budget—$396,789,950 for the two years, or $198,394,970 each year. The annual budget of the Department of Sanitation of the city of New York for 1985 was $396,338,544.

14. Gerard Manley Hopkins, "Peace," in *The Treasury of Christian Poetry,* comp. Lorraine Eitel et al. (Old Tappan, N.J.: Fleming H. Revell, 1982), 115.

15. Dorothee Sölle, *Revolutionary Patience,* trans. Rita and Robert Kimber (Maryknoll, N.Y.: Orbis Books, 1977).

16. Walter Brueggemann, *Living Toward a Vision: Biblical Reflection on Shalom* (Philadelphia: United Church Press, 1976), 156.

17. Ibid.

18. John Shea, *An Experience Named Spirit* (Chicago: Thomas More, 1983), 256.

19. James Breech, *The Silence of Jesus: The Authentic Voice of the Historical Man* (Philadelphia: Fortress Press, 1983), 61.

20. Martin Buber, *Israel and the World: Essays in a Time of Crisis* (New York: Schocken Books, 1948), 186, 199, 210.

6. A Race of Hawks, Owls, and Doves

1. Peter C. Craigie, *The Problem of War in the Old Testament* (Grand Rapids: Wm. B. Eerdmans, 1978); Millard C. Lind, *Yahweh Is a Warrior: The Theology of Warfare in Ancient Israel* (Scottdale, Penn.: Herald Press, 1980).

2. Peter Brock, *Pacifism in Europe to 1914* (Princeton: Princeton University Press, 1972).

3. Alistar Fox, *Thomas More, History and Providence* (New Haven, Conn.: Yale University Press, 1983), 131.

4. Esther C. Stine, "Would That Even Today You Knew the Things That Make for Peace," *Church and Society* 71 (January/February 1981): 27.

5. Arata Osada, comp., *Children of the A-Bomb* (Tokyo: Uchida Rokakuho Pub. House, 1959). See also Studs Terkel, *"The Good War": An Oral History of World War Two* (New York: Pantheon Books, 1984), 505-57.

6. Dale Aukerman, *Darkening Valley: A Biblical Perspective on Nuclear War* (New York: Seabury Press, 1981), 179.

7. Helge Heen, "A Response to: *In Defense of Creation*," letter dated November 17, 1986.

8. Aukerman, *Darkening Valley*, 179.

9. Charles C. West, "Forgiven Violence: Christian Responsibility Between Pacifism and Just War" in *Peace, Politics and the People of God*, ed. Paul Peachey (Philadelphia: Fortress Press, 1986), 71-94; see especially p. 77.

10. Peter B. Hinchliff, *Holiness and Politics* (Grand Rapids, Mich.: Wm. B. Eerdmans, 1982).

11. Jonathan Schell, "Reflections: The Abolition: I. Defining the Great Predicament," *New Yorker* (January 2, 1984): 37.

12. Quoted in Alan Bullock, "The Hidden Hero," *The New Republic* (September 22, 1986): 52.

13. As reproduced in John Howard Yoder's *What Would You Do?* (Scottdale, Penn.: Herald Press, 1983), 45-49.

14. As translated from Karl Barth, *Die Kirchliche Dogmatik*, Bd. 3, Teil 4 (Zurich: Evangelischer Verlag, 1951), 512.

15. Jenny Teichman, *Pacifism and the Just War: A Study in Applied Philosophy* (Oxford: Basil Blackwell, 1986), 1-9.